The Coastal Niger Delta

Environmental Development and Planning

Dr Michael Amaitari Niger

Order this book online at www.trafford.com
or email orders@trafford.com

Most Trafford titles are also available at major online book retailers.

Printed in the United States of America.

ISBN: 978-1-4669-1069-0 (sc)
ISBN: 978-1-4669-1071-3 (hc)
ISBN: 978-1-4669-1070-6 (e)

Library of Congress Control Number: 2012900133

Trafford rev. 01/11/2012

 www.trafford.com

North America & international
toll-free: 1 888 232 4444 (USA & Canada)
phone: 250 383 6864 ♦ fax: 812 355 4082

CONTENTS

FOREWORD

This research work and the results of our findings and conclusion are based on the Coastal Niger Delta as defined geographically or cartographically and not an administrative definition.

Geographically, the Coastal Niger Delta covers Rivers State, Bayelsa State and the south of the then Bendel State now Delta State. This is where we made our conclusions.

The regime of President Obansanjo's administration redefined and extended the Coastal Niger Delta in the year 2000. From this new definition, the Delta covers an area of about 70,000 km² making 7.5% of Nigeria's land mass instead of 36,296 km². This means that the Coastal Niger Delta is now officially made up of nine States: Bayelsa State, Delta State, Rivers State, Abia State, Akwa-Ibom State, Cross River State, Edo State, Imo State, and Ondo State with an altitude of over 400 m.

The work is meanly focused on the three states, Bayelsa, Delta (the southern part of the State) and Rivers as defined geographically, topographically or cartographically as the Niger Delta.

Dr M. A. Niger

FIGURES

PHOTOGRAPHY

Introduction

I.1: Showing a convex section of the Nun River in July with the sand bank almost submerged by the flood

I.2: The concave side of River opposite photo I.1

I.3: The vegetation along Rivers Forcados and Nun
  (a) Part of the forest on the bank of River Nun (freshwater zone)
  (b) Part of the forest on the bank of River Forcados (freshwater zone)

I.4: The vegetation of the transition zone

I.5: The vegetation of the brackish water zone

Chapter 1:

1.1: The landslide zone showing the affected trees and the flood plains (the convex bank)
  (a) The landslide.
  (b) The flood plains

1.2: Swamps: Typical situation of towns along Rivers Forcados and Nun
  (a) Built in a swampy area
  (b) North-West of the above area (a)
  (c) Erosion caused by run off (net flow)
  (d) Run off from precipitation (Rainfall)

1.3: A dwelling house affected by the phenomenon of erosion

Chapter 2:

2.1: The floods
  (a) A house built to avoid flooding
  (b) A house invaded by the floods at Amassoma

2.2: The levels of flooding (1988)
  (a) The layers of the flood levels (Yenagoa 1988)
  (b) The heights of the flood level (Amassoma 1988)

2.3: Flood and its disadvantages
  (a) Photo taken during a two hour heavy rainfall (Amassoma)
  (b) Municipal market invaded by floods (Yenagoa)

TABLES

GRAPHICS

Chapter 2:

2.1: The average monthly flow of various points of the River Niger (1979)

2.2: The evolution of daily floods and flood rates

(a) The daily average flow of River Niger at Onitsha (on 37 years of observations Nedeco)

(b) The evolution of the daily flooding at Amassoma recorded in September 1989

Chapter 3:

3.1: Average annual temperatures in the delta

3.2: Comparative: Annual precipitations.

3.3: The seasons of the Niger Delta

Chapter 9:

9.1: The evolution of the urban population (1930-1989) of the delta compared to that of the Country

9.2: The evolution of the urban population growth in the Niger Delta

The Eastern Niger Delta (the area of study)

The Northern Nigeria *(Consists of Nineteen States)*: *N°. 2-19, 23 +*
FCT:
2-Kebbi, 3-Sokoto, 4-Zamfara, 5-Katsina, 6-Kano, 7-Jigawa, 8-Yobe,
9-Borno, 10-Niger, 11-Kaduna, 12-Bauchi, 13-Gombe, 14-Kwara, 15-Koji,
FCT-Abuja, 16-Nassarawa, 17-Plateau, 18-Taraba, 19-Adamawa,
23-Benue

The Southern Nigeria *(Consists of Seventeen States)*: *N°. 1, 20-24,*
24-35:
1-Lagos, 20-Oyo, 21-Osun, 22-Ekiti, 24-Ogun, 25-Akwa Ibom, 26-Ondo,
27-Edo, 28-Delta, 29-Anambra, 30-Enugu, 31-Ebonyi, 32-Cross River,
33-Bayelsa, 34-Rivers, 35-Imo

(a) Map of Nigeria showing the Colonial division (North and South)
and Nigeria Today & the Coastal Niger Delta Region

States: *1-Rivers, 2-Bayelsa, 3-Delta, 4-Akwa Ibom, 5-Abia, 6-Imo, 7-Cross River, 8-Edo, 9-Ondo*

(b) Map showing the 9 States administratively considered as part of the Coastal Niger Delta.

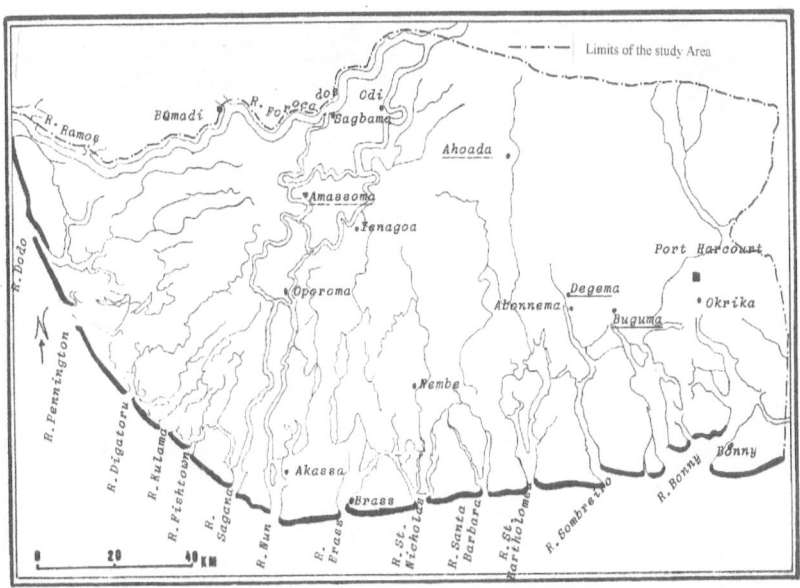

(c) Limits of the region of the Delta studied with some major cities/towns.

Fig I.1: Definition and the region studied: Bayelsa and Rivers States.

INTRODUCTION

The Research in the field of development and planning of the Niger Delta is in its infancy, but it is possible to identify a set of qualitative and topographic features of the environment specific to the Region.

In fact, the principal problems facing development and planning the towns in the Niger Delta are topographic, geographic and human.

I.1. The subject of the theme of study

We have been conscious for several years by the problems of flooding, erosion and other natural constraints. These are our experiences and our knowledge of the Delta region. The influence that these scourges exercise on the region is as much as human as the topography of the environment, morphology of the towns, the lifestyle and economic activities, diseases: cholera, malaria, eye disease, hepatitis B and other diseases yet unknown, but immerging in the Delta affecting its inhabitants.

In fact, the Niger Delta is long been considered an amphibious zone, because of its very low altitude above sea level, 20 metres at the most (more than two-third), compounded by the multitude of creeks, marshes and swamps. These special topographic and hydrological conditions characterizing the Delta limit the extension planning. It is however, for us, not only interesting to study the region, but also highlight opportunities for expansion and planning the towns and cities in the Delta. This will be a development that takes into account the local economic conditions. It will also reflect on the technical tools related to this development.

About two-thirds of the entire Niger Delta (36,269 km²) are below 15 m altitude above sea level. This resulted to an uneven development and spatial planning of the towns and cities in the Delta as compared to other cities and towns in other States in the country. Why? Because the

Authorities at that time (the then Government of the Eastern Region) believed that the Niger Delta cannot be developed. Today, due to the pressure from the Delta people these pre-judgements are phasing out, but there is yet more to be done by the Federal Government, since The Niger Delta is the bread winner of the Nation "The Pride of the Nation" (Rivers State) and the Glory of all lands (Bayelsa State).

The policy pursued in the Delta Regional planning has involved in recent years to promote the idea that the entire south and the annual flood affected areas cannot be intensively developed. This idea originated from the then Government of the Eastern Region and continued until the creation of the Rivers State in 1967. The idea still survives, but in another form, and Authorities.

However, the programs of urban development have not integrated the particularities of the entire Delta. Much of this uneven development is due to the political authorities, Federal Government, and the different State Governments in the Delta. Furthermore, no study focused on urban expansion has been done taking into account the peculiarities of the Delta environment. The studies to date are on the morphology and the navigability of the river (NEDECO), the rural development related to agriculture (Niger Delta Basin Authority, Ministry of Works & Transport) etc

However, the Institute for flood, erosion, soil reclamation and transport[1], with the assistance of NDBDA and the Ministry of Works and Transport (Port Harcourt) made few studies. These are projects of soil reclamation, erosion etc (on the eastern Niger Delta).

There are however, a mismatch between the management programs and the needs identified at the town level in the zones. This makes the region (Delta), a typical example of under-developed and most neglected regions in the country despite its position as the bread winner (The oil producing Region).

Thus, this issue seems particularly aimed at the technical and economical solutions compatible with all the problems topographic, geographic and human resources identified in the region including issues of extension of its cities and towns.

---

[1]   Rivers State University of Science and Technology-Port Harcourt, Rivers

I.2. The issue of our research

The natural phenomena such as, flood, erosion, topography, and the morphology of the Delta present many problems to development and urban expansion.

In fact, the existence of many creeks, streams, swamps has resulted to the concentration of all development projects and utilities on the State Capitals, it suburbs, some local government headquarters and other towns that could be reached by road communication from the Capital of the State, Port Harcourt in the Eastern Delta, Warri, Sapele in the western Delta. In other words, no action or serious research was carried out to remedy the conditions in the other areas of the Delta. The planning policies and development projects of the western part of the Delta is much more developed and more equipped than the Eastern Delta[1]. Today, the Niger Delta has two definitions: physical or geographical and administrative. The administrative Niger Delta is larger and beyond the physical and morphological boundaries of the Region of the Niger Delta: Political or administrative manipulation?

However, some geographers believed that the Delta could be developed, but some parts and not the whole Delta. Indeed, the northern area which is essentially the fresh water area. A report made by NEDECO (1966) shows that the Delta can be developed, but at a high cost. This idea is also has been Government concern since the dawn of independence, but no serious programs were made to follow up these results.

An Organization called the Niger Delta Development Board (NDDB) was created by the Federal Government. Its mission was practically on an economic and development of agriculture (Appendices III), but closed after the creation of Rivers States in the Eastern Niger Delta in 1967. This Organization was replaced on the 3rd August 1976 by the Niger Delta Basin Development Authority (NDBDA). This new Government Agency's mission is to undertake research studies on the development of towns in the Delta. Some works has already been done. Other works have been done by the Ministry of Works & Transport and the Institute of flood, erosion, soil reclamation and Transport, Rivers State University of

---

[1]   Under the then administration of western Region, Mid-West Region and Bendel State, now a State-Delta State.

Science and Technology-Port Harcourt. These two Organizations work in association with the NDBDA.

Therefore, it is interesting to ponder more specifically on the problems of expansion and urbanization policy of towns in the Delta. This should incorporate the phenomenon of the fight against flooding, erosion, and transport.

The policy pursued with regard to land use by the Federal Government in the recent years has been to favour the construction of hydropower plants to bring the country's energy independence. The construction of a dam at Kanji (fig 2.1) allowed the clipping of floods in the delta. Two others dams are to be built: Jebba dam (103 Km downstream from Kanji) and the one at Shiroro at Kaduna River. However, this construction is not part of a development project intended to take into account the problems specific of the Niger Delta: the problems of flooding, erosion and so on.

In fact, the elements that characterize almost all the towns in the delta are: The importance of the great sandy plains, the multitude of sand banks on the convex[1] of the river banks, channel . . . The plains are flooded during the rainy season, up to 25 m high above the lowest river water level in dry season at Amassoma, on the nun river (tributary); Odi, on the Nun river; Patani and Sagbema, on the forcados river.

In the plains beyond the couvet (plains) of Amassoma and some plains on the rivers nun and forcados, the height of flooding ranges from 1.5 m to 10 m, which threatens the villages, cities, towns, crops, roads and communication. The overflow of rivers across the towns is common.

I.3. The presentation of the Niger delta

The Niger Delta is a low-lying plain with an altitude of 20 m at the maximum and covers a wide area (1). Nevertheless, it covers an area of 36,269 km , but it is sparsely populated: Approximately 5,069,000 people[2] with a population density of 140 people per square kilometre. It occupies most of the Nigerian continental shelf which plunges down from Lagos to Cameroon (fig2.1). It lies between the longitudes 5° West and 6°

---

[1]   It is the largest, compared to other Deltas in Africa. Population estimated to the nearest thousand.

[2]   Projection of the 1963 census in 1989

04' East; latitudes 8°48' North and 4°7' South. It is therefore, limited by the Benin River to the west and the Bonny River in the east (fig 1.10).

The two principal Rivers (Forcados and Nun) of the Niger Delta, resulting from the division of River Niger flow through the Delta and into the Atlantic Ocean (fig I.2). These two Rivers, Forcados and Nun, divide forming other rivers such as river Ramos, Sangana . . . Then with other rivers, Benin, Brass, Bonny, the creeks, the streams forming a combination of labyrinth of rivers and lagoons. It forms a series of discontinuous islands that allows navigation parallel along the sea from Lagos to Rio del Ray (Cameroon). As described by Winwood Reale (1867) "*It is the Venice of West Africa*" However, the Delta has a large number of sheltered sites favourable for the construction of ports. We can already cite historical ports, such as that of Bonny, Brass, Forcados, Port Harcourt, Warri . . .

The Niger Delta has for centuries played an important role in the economy of the country. During the pre-colonial period, its people have acted as intermediaries between Europeans and traders within the country. From 17th to 18th centuries, the combined trading activities in the Niger Delta made its ports one of the most important centres of slave trade in the Atlantic coast of West Africa.

With the introduction of palm oil trade in the 19th century, its ports have exported more palm oil than the rest of the West Africa. But the importance of the Delta's economy is now the presence of crude oil, due to the geographical structures, geological, hydrological forms that characterize it.

In the geographical point of view, the Niger Delta is divided into three physical zones (fig 1.2):

1. The Northern zone which is drier and higher.
2. The marshy, mangrove or swamp zone of the (middle belt) South of Northern zone.
3. The region of the narrow strip of barrier islands that boarder the Atlantic Ocean.

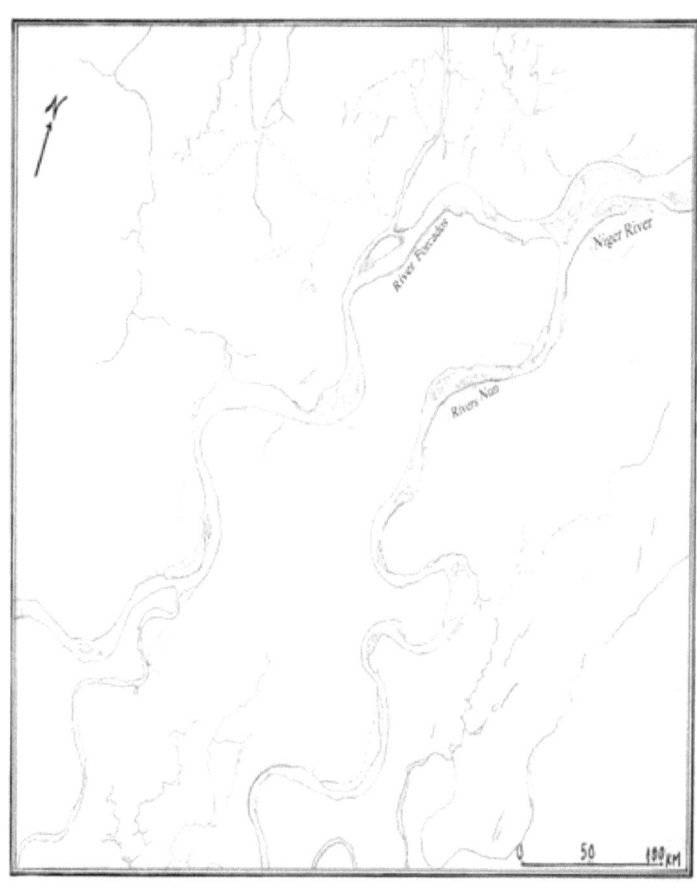

Fig I.2: Sources of Rivers Forcados and Nun

I.3.1. <u>The main Rivers of Niger Delta.</u>

The Rivers Forcados and Nun (fig I.2) are the two principal rivers of the Niger Delta. These two rivers flow through the Delta brutally carrying an important quantities of alluvium (silt) and sediments to the interior of the Delta during the rainy seasons; River Forcados debits about 2015 m3 while the Nun River debits 1,400 m3.

Although these two Rivers have resulted from the division of the same river (Niger), their flow rate and volume of flood, erosion . . . make the difference between them.

I.3.1.1. <u>River Nun</u>

The Nun River covers a distance of approximately 165 km from its source Niger River (fig I.3) to the Atlantic Ocean. It passes through three types of separate waters: fresh water, zone de transition (*mixed water-fresh and salt waters*), and the Brackish water (fig 1.2).

The Nun has two main problems: (a)-during the dry season: Due to the shallowness of certain parts of the Rivers and falling trees in the river due to landslide, presents risks to navigation. (b)-during the rainy season: flooding and an intensification of erosion during the beginning of the floods.

These problems are mainly in the areas of freshwater and in the transition zone.

Topographically, the river Nun is characterized by sand banks (Photo I.1) on the convex side, while the concave side[1] is characterized by falling trees from the landslide (Photo I.2 and figs I.4 and I.5). Indeed, the landslide of the river Bank (cliff) decreases when approaching the area of the Brakishwater zone[2], except behind the coastal barrier islands where the flow rate is extremely high at each change of tide[3]. In the transition zone, sand is rarely seen above the water level either at ebb-tide or flood-tide and gentle slops on the two bangs of the river (concave and convex).

---

[1]   Given the part convex. See also fig I.3.

[2]   Flood and ebb tides.

[3]   Even during the rainy season.

Fig.I.3: The course of River Nun and its main tributaries

Photo I.1: Showing a convex section of the Nun River in July with the sand bank almost submerged by the flood.

(a)Landslide on the River Bank

(b) Landside at the River bank.

Photo I.2: The concave side of the river opposite Photo I.1.

The bank of the landslides: This morphology was observed throughout the Forcados and the Nun rivers in the freshwater and in the transition zones (less noticeable here).

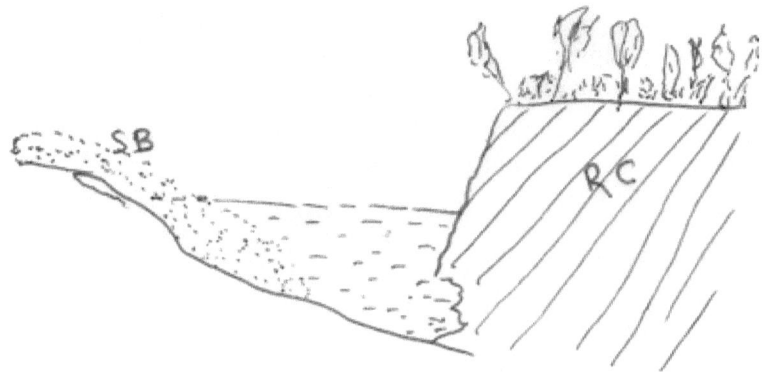

SB=Sandbank; RC=Sandy Clay soil (active erosion/landslide zone)
Fig I.4: Cross section of River Nun (Section A-A).

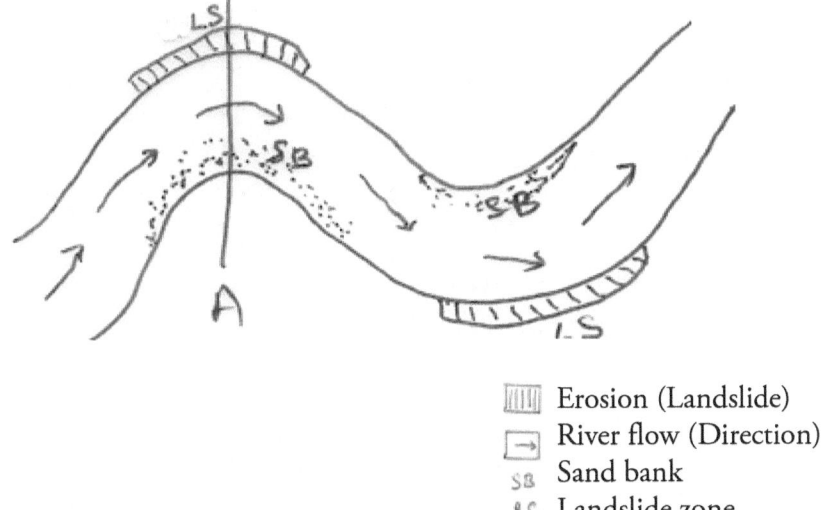

▦	Erosion (Landslide)
→	River flow (Direction)
SB	Sand bank
RC	Landslide zone

Fig I.5: River Nun view from above.

I.3.1.2. The Forcados River (fig I.8)

Forcados River covers a distance of about 125 km from the apex of it, flowing through the Delta to the Atlantic Ocean. The physical characteristics of the two Rivers (Forcados and Nun) are the same. However, the difference lies on the fact that the problems are greater in the case of Forcados than those of River Nun. In addition, the Forcados receives more volume of water from the River Niger; 59 % of the volume, while the Nun receives only 41 % (NEDECO 1961). This explains the importance of the problems of erosion, flooding, flow rate, volume and the depth of the River than that of Nun.

I.4. Settlement patterns and vegetation along the Forcados and Nun Rivers

I.4.1. The Sites:

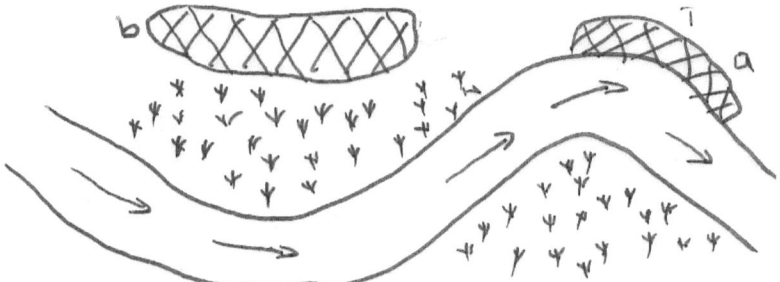

(a). Town/Village located on a bank with less affect by landslide.
(b). A town/Village behind flood plains.

[flood plains symbol]	Flood plains
[separated settlement symbol]	Separated settlement (from the main town)
[main town symbol]	Main town (Area of first settlement)
a	Cliff
b	High-flood plain
LS	Landslide

[Key for figs I.6 & I.7]

Fig I.6: General pattern of sites. More frequent type of sites in the Niger Delta.

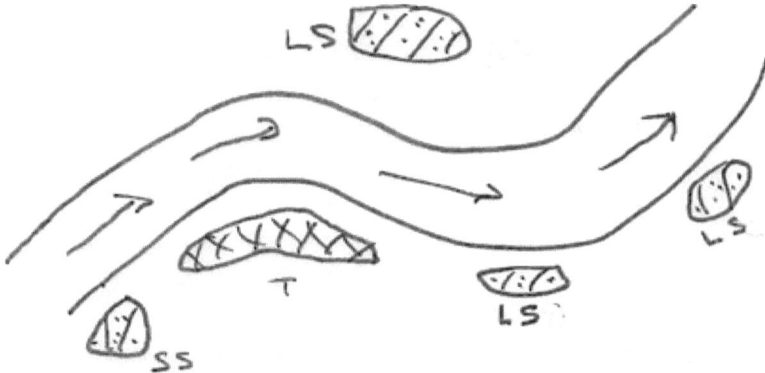

Fig I.7: System of settlements on the Forcados River.

Fig I.8: The course of River Forcados and its Tributaries

I.5. The vegetation

In an obvious connection with the hydrology, the Niger delta has varied vegetation in different regions or zones: freshwater region vegetation, transitional region vegetation, and the brackish water vegetation (mangroves region). But the limits of typical formations are also depending on the nature of the soil. The areas studied in particular, covers the central part of the delta (Bayelsa and Rivers) with the two principal Rivers (Forcados and Nun) and their tributaries down to the Atlantic Ocean.

The vegetation in the freshwater area which is essentially the upper delta is characterized by an infinite number of billowing tops, thick curtains of green along the rivers, streams, wetlands, presence of large trunks and buttresses of diameters impressive. The tree leaves are large and green foothills and stilt roots grafted to trunk to a good height from the ground (Photo I.3). But the vegetation does not make the same association everywhere. A slightest modification of the milieu (soil, slope), favours certain species and banish others, especially in flood plains and bases dominated by grasses and a few shafts from February to August. Indeed, several plants species form permanent associations such as diopiros, the niangon (tarries utilis), large sedges mopania, mahogany (khaya ivorensis), iroko (chlorophora excelsa) and raffia (raffia spp) etc

(a) Part of the forest on the bank of River Nun
(freshwater zone).

(b) Part of the forest on the River Forcados
(Freshwater zone).

Photo I.3: The vegetation on the banks of Rivers.
(It may be noted that the components of the vegetation along the two Rivers are the same).

Therefore, the plant mass, generally in the upper part of the Niger delta liner has a profusion of trees whose height ranges from 15 to 60 m and woody vines with large diameters are numerous, changes in vegetation of the Niger delta is even more interesting in the region that we call "the transition zone" is a mixing zone of freshwater and brackish water vegetation area (Photo I.4). The crossing from one vegetation to another is observed by its diminution of the types of vegetation characterizing one zone gradually giving rise to the nest zone (Photo I.4), such as from fresh water vegetation to mangrove. On the River Nun, the transition zone is clearly observable around 1.5 km from the town of Peremabiri towards the South, to village of Lasukugbene where it ends[1].

This zone covers about 2 to 3 km wide between the upper and middle delta. The vegetation of the rest of the delta (Photo I.5)-middle and lower delta is dominated by mangroves.

However, we can conclude that there are particular Plant species found in the delta and are consist of mangroves, oil palm trees, and raphia palm trees, multitudes of medicinal (homeopathic) plants.

---

[1]   Observations were made by cruising along the Rivers, Creeks and on foot at some villages and towns (Peremobiri, Lasuku-gbene, Sagbama, Ahoada, Patani etc).

(a) The end, from the South of the transition zone
(River Nun)

(b) The beginning, from the North of the transition zone
(River Nun)

Photo I.4: The vegetation of the transition zone.
(Note the presence of palm trees and mangroves. We can also notice the mixture of trees including the oil palm trees and mangroves)

Photo I.5: The vegetation of the brackish water zone.

Note the palm trees and disappeared completely from other trees of the freshwater zone. Also the complete domination of mangroves and other vegetation in the brackish water zone

I.6. The limit of the case study area.

We adopted as the limit of our research, an area of 19,049 Km² (about 53%), almost the entire region of the delta (fig I.1), limited geographically to the West by the Rivers Forcados-Ramos and the Bonny River on the East.

Indeed, the source of River Forcados to the town of Bomadi and Ramos River, continue following the river to the Atlantic Ocean to the west on the one hand and on the other hand, the Bonny River to Atlantic Ocean to the North, the lower limit of the Niger River (fig 1.2) and South by the Atlantic Ocean. Our limits include the mangrove, the transition zone, the sub-littoral, including the River Nun and eleven[1] other rivers (fig 1.10) between the rivers Forcados-Ramos and river Bonny, and the terraces of old and the area of the delta brown soils, flat dense forest of the northern extension of the alluvial plains north-west of the Niger River flood plain.

---

[1] The Rivers Dodo, Pennington, Digatoru, Koluama, Fish Town, Sagama, Brass, St. Nicholas, Santa Barbara, St. Bartholomew, Sambreiro.

In addition, we used the criteria provided by the distribution of the Ijaw and Ikwerre people[1]. They give way to other populations including Igbos beyond the limits on the north-east. Indeed, the southern boundary and the north-eastern limits correspond to the north-east of Rivers State. With in the limits, our research covers a total population of about 3,882,000 inhabitants (projection 1989). The delta is made in its entire flood plains, mangroves swamps and islands with a low population density. The population density is about 204 persons per square kilometres.

The urban population is 922,000 (23.76%) while the rural population is approximately 2,960,000 (1989 Projection) (76.24%). The originality of the delta population is that they involve themselves in some rural cottage industries and trade, but not farming except the groups of populations in the North-East which are mainly farmers: Ikwerres, Ogonis, and Abuas etc. The rest are fishermen and does a little farming, mainly for home consumption and are in the southern part of the delta. A town in the Niger Delta by definition will therefore have no numerical value.

The Niger Delta is the most populous and the largest delta in comparison with other deltas in Africa: the Zambezi, the internal Niger delta, the Nile delta, the Volta, Ouéme etc. For example: the Zambezi Delta (Guru 1971) is populated by Farmers on the barrier beaches and ridges with a density of 15h Km². The Inland Niger Delta is populated by 346,000 inhabitants and an area of 13,200 square kilometres. This gives a population density of 26.3 habitants per kilometres square (Prof Gallais) which has not been more than the vast delta plain in the dry areas of adjacent and the same altitude. The Inland Niger Delta is an under populated delta.

The Coastal Niger Delta had a population density of 20 inhabitants before the creation of the States (Rivers, Bayelsa and Delta States). This density is largely obsolete today. If other deltas in Africa like Ouémé, Nile, Volta had a density of 150.60, because their superficies are less than that of the coastal Niger Delta.

---

[1]   Including Ogba/Egbema and the Ekpeye minority groups North-East (Area of the research). Fishermen in the south, Farmers in the North-East and divers professions in the North and at the west (mostly traders). The Eastern Part of the Delta.

Environmental constraints

The vegetation and hydrograph of Nigeria identifies three main parts: The Sudanese savannah, the Guinean zone and the Equatorial zone. In the latter, is the particular vegetation of the Coastal Niger Delta and are made up of mangroves, Palm oil trees, raphia palms etc.

An aerial view shows the landscape of the Coastal Niger delta, small irregular spots of brown bright crescent-shaped patches. These are the settlements (the towns and villages). These towns and villages are generally characterized by a main road along a river, lake or creek with houses constructed along the river (photo I.6) or around the Lake or passing through the middle of the town.

The hydrograph is organized into five basins of four relieves from the various rivers before emptying it into the Atlantic Ocean. Indeed, the country is crossed by two major rivers: the first River Niger from the North-West and the second, the River Benue from North-East. The River Niger rises from the high mountains of Guinea, while the River Benue is from Mount Cameroon. These two rivers meet at Lokoja, after receiving the waters of various other rivers and streams (tributaries). They flow into the Gulf of Guinea (former bight of Biafra) passing through a labyrinth of creeks, rivers streams and lagoons forming the Coastal Niger Delta.

In fact, the main topographical features of the Coastal Niger Delta are dominated by Islands, swamps, flood plains, water and mangroves. An observation on aerial photographs of the Coastal Niger delta shows that the wider unity of the area is amphibious brackish water (saline swamps), the low alluvial flood plains, the tidal estuaries and so on. These are the main constraints facing planning and expanding the towns and which favours the settlement of the towns in length along mostly the levee of the rivers etc. Secondly, the first settlers of the Niger Delta were fishermen which probably suggested their settling grounds: either near to their fishing ground or fishing grounds that later developed into towns.

These facts lead us to analyse the topographical constraints for planning and developing the Coastal Niger Delta for possible solutions to the question. Knowing the problem is the first step to founding a solution. As a physician first diagnosis his patient from the symptoms for an appropriate treatment, so are we to look critically into these natural obstacles (constraints) in chapters one through five for possible solutions.

However, there are solutions to these problems and natural obstacles to promote the possibilities of expansion and development of towns in the Delta. Our first attempt is to see into the conditions and obstacles (constraints) in the Niger delta. This will lead us to stress on the analysis to determine the issues to the problems of development and expansion of the towns in the Coastal delta and its environment.

This volume is meant to answer only one question (*without solutions yet)* "what are the problems of developing and planning the Coastal Niger Delta?" We will make specific case studies on towns chosen from the three geo-morphological zones of the Delta. In those volumes (case studies), that we will propose our technical-economic and human solutions specific to each the zone.

Chapter 1

The Development and Planning constraints in the Niger Delta

A delta is defined as an alluvial plain[1] that forms when a river enters a body of water[2]. It is characterized by the existence of alluvial sandy clay alternating with sediments. However, the development of a delta depends on sediment supplied which must be faster than the sediment dispersal mechanism acting in the basin.

In fact, the system (fig 1.1) of the delta plain is composed of (a) **upper delta** which is the region of the alluvial plains characterized by predominantly fluvial deposits and (b) the **Lower delta plains** are the plains of the lower delta located in the area of confrontational rivers and marine activities. The second part is below the upper limit of tidal delta say the front (the lower delta front), but we are interested only in maritime deltas. Nevertheless, we distinguish two groups of deltas. The first group of deltas are characterized by high accumulation rivers and are lobbies that indicate a progression. The Mississippi delta is part of this group, but with more rapidly progressing levees projecting the arms forward to the sea (fig 1.1B (b) (c))[3].

In fact, it is all round the globe that we have these types of deltas[4]. The largest deltas are those of the most abundant inflow of rivers, such as the Mississippi (34,000 km²) and Niger (17,600 km²). The sediment is

---

[1] Resulting from the accumulation by sedimentation
[2] An ocean, an inland sea, a lake etc.
[3] Which gives the digitised deltas (Mississippi)?
[4] Of sea tidal deltas (Mississippi, Niger . . .) or without sea (the Nile, the Tiber . . .), inland seas (the inland Niger Delta) or lake (Ethiopia).

characterized by the power of the delta. However, the larger deltas reach several hundred metres. For example: a range of 1000 m of new deposits for Mississippi.

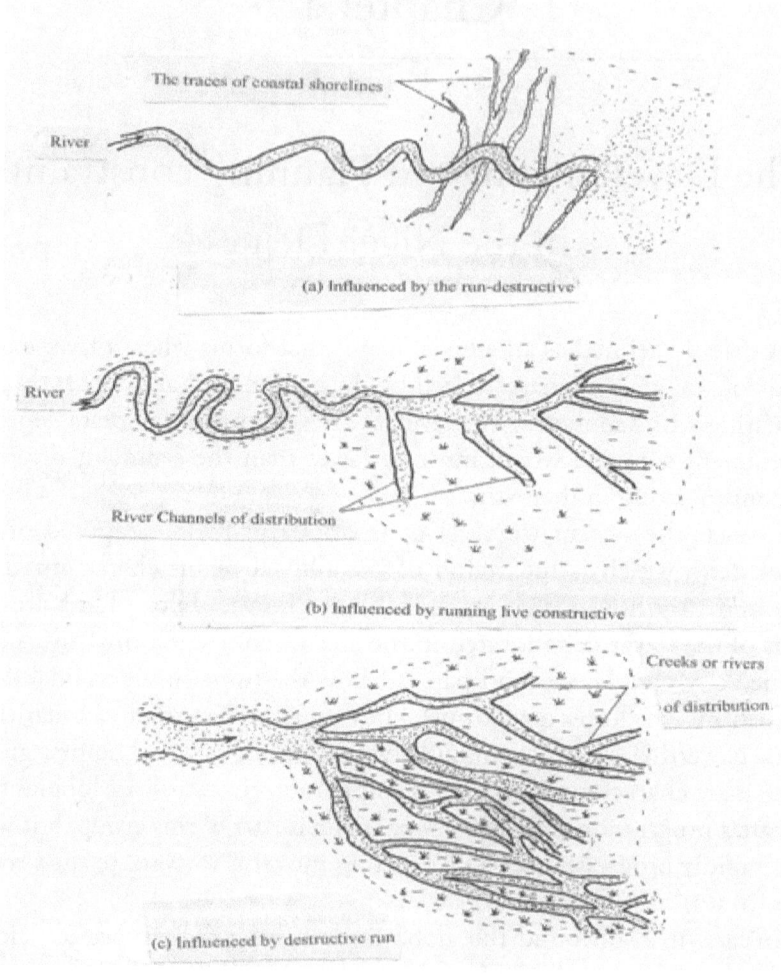

(a) Influenced by the run-destructive

(b) Influenced by running live constructive

(c) Influenced by destructive run

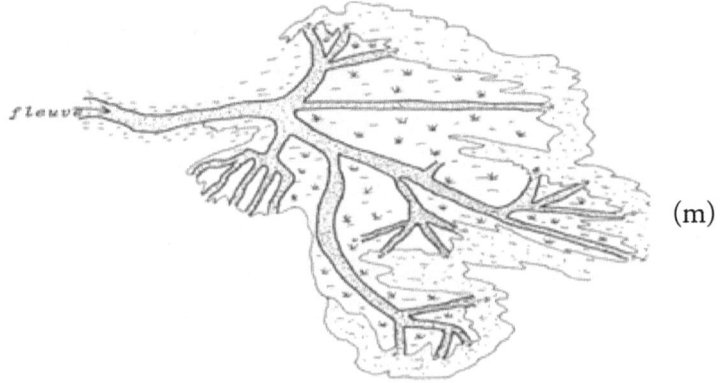

(m)

(m)=The mouths of the distributaries

Fleuve = River

(d) Influenced by constructive run (very active)

(A) Type of Deltas and the topography of their fluvial deposits

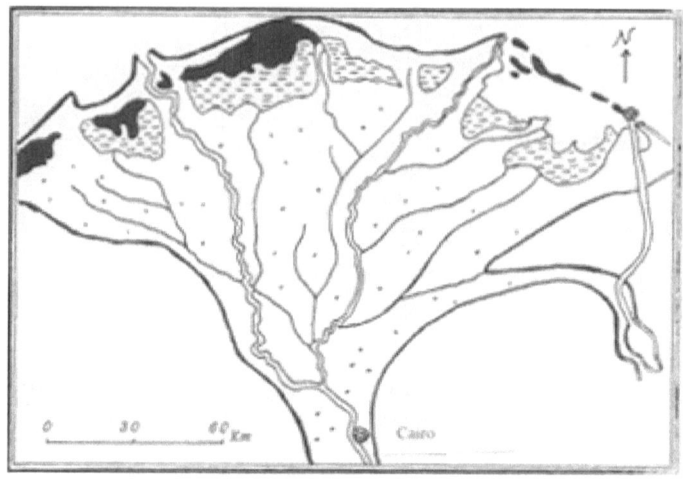

(a) The Nile Delta.

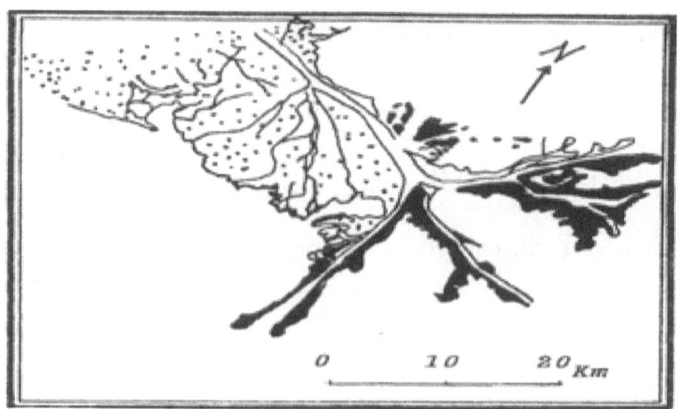

(b) The Mississippi Delta. Fingered Part.

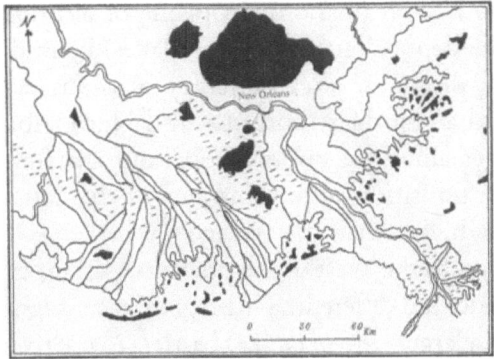

(c) The fingered Mississippi delta. Examples of coastal deltas.

(B) Examples of Coastal Deltas.

Fig 1.1: Types, topography and nature of the formations of River and Maritime Deltas.

1.1.0. The Principal morphological units of the Coastal Niger Delta.

The Niger delta occupies the major part of the continental shelf down-plunging from Nigeria to Cameroon. It is however, limited by the Benin River to the West, Cross river to the East including the area of the coast where the mountain plunges into the Atlantic Ocean. It covers an area of 36,269 km² covering three States (Rivers, Bayelsa [1] (fig 1.2) and the southern part of Delta State at the West.

The two main river that originated from River Niger (Forcados and Nun), passing through the delta, with other rivers such as Benin, Brass, Bonny, Sambreiro etc formed a labyrinth of creeks, rivers and islands to the Atlantic Ocean (introduction).

When we entered the delta by River Nun (and then by River Forcados), we found first a very simple relief and rather limited plains. The river

---

[1]   This place occupies the eastern Niger delta (adjustment made by the Federal Government 2000).

established on both sides of the main plains of altitudes from 4 to 15 m dominating the depressions (swamps or lakes) behind the Rivers. The cushion does not disappear after the entry of the rivers, but continues to the border, and along their (Forcados and Nun) tributaries. One can follow these ridges along the rivers throughout the freshwater[1] and the upper part of the transition zone. This part of the delta is characterized partly by altitudes higher than the average (20 m).

To the East and to the West of the previous section, extend the regions whose characteristics are different. This region has a higher altitude (from 15 to 20 m), with a larger strip of land as barriers to the river currents. These cover the area of high and middle delta that are intensively cultivated[2].

The Southern region is a low region including the transition and sub-littoral zones. These regions are Warri, Bomadi, etc (on the west) and Okubie, Bakana (on the East) down to the Atlantic Ocean. It covers an area of 22,320 ha. Low altitude area (4 to 8 m).

The Niger Delta consists of three geomorphologic units (fig 1.2): (a) Behind a chain of barrier islands of two types of sand ripples. (b) The flat tidal land characterized by mangrove Swamps and (c) Creeks, flooded trees and flood plains.

---

[1]   This area is called "well drained land" forest and covers an area of 9.75 ha

[2]   The portion of freshwater at Forcados and Nun rivers. Except the North-East and North-West (the West of Forcados and Nun).

▨ Upper Delta (River Flood Plains)
▨ The Middle Delta (swamps & mangroves)
▨ The coastal Zone
▨ The Barrier Islands

Fig. 1.2: The Geomorphologic Regions of the Coastal Niger Delta

The reticulated water system and the marsh are probably due to the stabilization of the sedimentary deposit, the mangrove and the manner in which they are located.

The main geomorphologic units are therefore, the flood plains, the mangroves and the chains of barrier islands (fig 1.2). The total area of these plains is about 8,400 km². The upper part rises to the North. It is about 20 m above sea level.

The Niger River is the main source of the flooding of the coastal Niger Delta. Two other rivers in the east and west of the plains flank the river Niger. The lower part of the plains is much broader (wider) with a gentle slope (1 to 0.5 %) in the coast. The river Niger divides at this level into several creeks and rivers forming a large meanders. The distribution of sediments and floods of the Niger River in the many creeks and rivers, are uneven, but the rivers Nun and Forcados have the highest proportions (table 1.1). The creeks and rivers are flanked by natural levees that descend on to swamp forest.

The mangrove swamps are flat vegetations with dominance of red mangrove (rizophora racemoza) except in the rivers and creeks. The area occupied by the rivers and creeks, however, is minimal compared to that occupied by the red mangrove. Change in tidal range is between 1 and 2 metres. The total area of mangroves is about 9000 km² which extends from the Benin river region in the west to the estuary of Calabar, Rio del Ray to the east. A maximum width of 30 to 40 km is reach on the flank of the delta where the marsh filled the angle between the boundary of the flood plain and terrace of earlier sediments. The contact between the flat flood plains and the marsh is cashed deep into the bay.

Rivers	Flood Volume Brackish water m3/s	Flood Volume Fresh water m3/s
Forcados	14,822	2,015
Nun	10,300	1,400
Brass	16,670	460
St. Nicholas	4,700	60
Santa Barbara	5,320	Negligible
St Bartholomew	5,070	200
Sambreiro	10,530	196
New Calabar	8.800	Negligible
Bonny	18,750	Little
Andoni	6,990	Negligible
Opobo	6,990	23

Source: NEDECO 1961

Table 1.1: The liquid flow of the Coastal Niger Delta
(*East of the delta*)

1.1.1. The solid debris carried by the Niger River

The solid debris[1] transported to the coastal Niger delta is Palaeozoic[2] and various rocks in their path from the high mountains of Guinea. At the confluence of the rivers Niger and Benue at Lokoja, the Niger River carries a total of 300,000 m3 of debris per year and approximately 460,000 m3 per year of elements in suspension (alluvial sand and clay) while River Benue transports about 600,000 m3 of alluvial sand and Coarse per year and suspended parts of about 11 million m3. This makes a total of 165,000 m3 of solid debris carried to the delta.

In fact, 65% of all solid debris carried by the two rivers deposited in the delta only 35% reaches the Atlantic Ocean. It seems that very few of these 35% gets into the ocean. The rest is deposited behind probably the barrier islands. The slope length upstream of Niger Delta[3] is characterized by a slope of 1:1500.

The average is between 1:800 and 1:400. But the platform of the delta slope varies between 1:2000 and 1:4000. Note that the slopes of 1:5 to 1:10 augment when there is erosion (Beach). However, the typical slopes of the Coastal Niger Delta are from 1:100 to 1:50. The dynamics of the Niger Delta[4] is characterized by the presence of natural rivers and coastal processes.

More than 6% of the delta is (+1.7 million ha) formed by Phyto-stable upland and flood plains and more than 6.9% of the delta consists of a medium tendency to instability. This medium is found along streams, rivers and estuaries. The party formed by mangroves occupy 76 % of the delta, an area of over 21.33 million ha and 7.41 million ha of lowlands North of Port Harcourt (the soil is exhausted). The whole region seems to be a region of instability.

Nevertheless, more than 3.39 million ha which are formed by the barrier beaches tend to stability, if they are degraded by oil or tourism activities that are developing in the recent years. It should be noted that the coastal Niger delta of which the advancing deltaic margins accompanied by a great mobility of their coastlines. The advance is made at variable

---

[1] Sediments (solid debris) are mostly medium and coarse sands.
[2] A time of dramatic geological, climatic, and evolutionary change
[3] From Onitsha to the delta.
[4] Percentages and data correspond to the eastern part of the Delta.

speeds [1] that benefit both massive inflows of sediments[2] and the extension of platforms underwater.

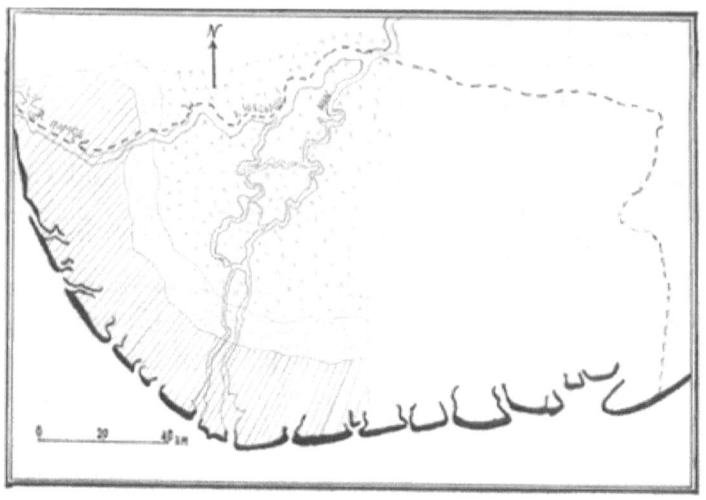

Plains

▨ Floods-River (Fresh water zone)

▧ Transition Zone (River & Tidal)

▨ Tidal (Brackish water zone)

Fig 1.3: The types of flood plains.

---

[1] Part of west to east: 70 to 100 m per year.
[2] About 1000 m3 of recent filings

1.1.2. The internal morphology of the Coastal Niger Delta.

1.1.2.1. The Flood Plains.

Let us consider first instance the general construction of the flood plains. They are formed by the river basins and the extent of the flat terrain.

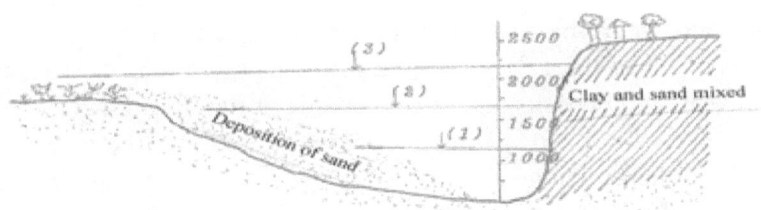

(1) Water level at low tide. Dry season.
(2) Water level at flood tide (high tide). Dry season.
(3) Water level in the rainy season (flood).
(a).A section of River Nun showing different levels of tides and flood levels on the banks.

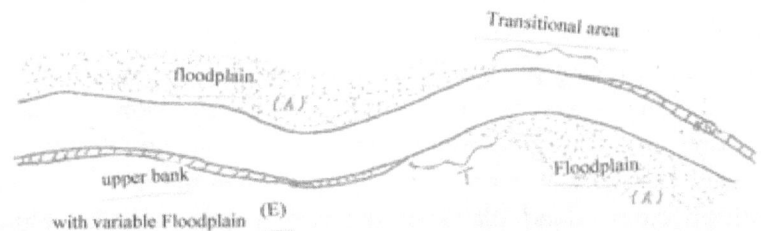

(E): Zone of erosion.   (A): Zone of alluvial deposits.
(b). Alternating levees and the flood plains.

Fig.1.4: The general morphology of the Rivers in the Upper Delta (E.g. Forcados and Nun)

During maturity, the bed of the basin becomes wider. This is due to lateral erosion. This is affected by migrants in the meandering direction of flow of the rivers and steams in which an active deposition starts on the bench covered with meanders[1]. Eventually, the entire bed of the basin is affected by the meanders on both sides of the basin.

After the stage of maturity, the river begins to overflow with a deposit of silt and mud on the bed of the basin which indicates the final stage of development of the flood plain[2].

The banks of the meanders are of variable heights. That is, those on one side of the basin (river banks) can be higher than the bank opposite (side) to it[3]. They are not paired with those newly deposited. In the case of two major rivers in the delta, this variation of the height difference is well defined and distinct as it is in the area of freshwater and brackish water areas. There are in the areas of freshwater floodplains, a very gentle slope into the river bed (fig 1.3). The flood plains are often characterized by the presence of sand deposits on the convex side of the River bank.

In fact, the flood plains are characterized by the presence of amphibious herbs that go down to the water level during high tides in the dry season. The minimum width of the flood plain is 800 m (4). There is an area which ranges from 50 to 100 metres (along the river), we called this "transitional bank zone". This area is characterized by the presence of vegetation that characterizes the flood plaints and the bank (with variable heights). It is often, characterized by presence of trees from the banks of the rivers (photo 1.1 and fig 1.6). It is this side that is generally affected by the landslide at the beginning of the rainy season. Unfortunately, these are the ideal locations for towns to escape the annual flooding.

The transition or passage between two adjacent shores (flood plains and high River banks) is done with a gradual reduction of small trees and grasses until they gives way completely to large and tall trees. At the end of the new zone, the processes repeat itself in the reverse order. The deposition covers flood plains of the two tributaries-Rivers Nun and Forcados. In the freshwater[4] limits, these tributaries develop more and

---

[1]   Cf. fig 1.9: mechanism of erosion by the river Nun

[2]   See the flood: Transition zone of fresh and brackish water.

[3]   It should be noted that the migration of meanders in the direction of the river flow and continue all literal and vertical erosion. It is quite possible that most of the first elements deposited are removed by this action, but the remaining portion will form the terrace above the new flood plain that grows (accumulating).

[4]   From 20 to 50 m, but sometimes very abruptly, giving rise to small trees.

more in this area and the depths of the creeks and streams rarely exceed 9.75 m in the dry season[1].

(a) The Landslide.
(*Note the trees lost in this phenomenon*).

(b).The flood plain.
(*Note the sand bank that building up in the opposite the active landslide zone*)

Photo 1.1: The landslide zone showing the affected trees and the flood plain (the convex bank)

---

[1]   The southern limit of the fresh water zone.

1.1.2.2. The erosion of the river bed.

The beds of canals are often dry which allows us to comments on the mechanism of digging. Indeed, the walls of the banks bare, large bulky and coarse blocks from the eroding bed and bank walls of the river dig hollow cylindrical cavities. The digging continues with awhirl at the bottom of the cylindrical cavities, putting sand, pebbles rounded in motion. This represents the tools water uses to drill. We have done the same observations to study the model on the river Nun threshold mechanisms of erosion by the river Nun[1].

In fact, it is very rare we have an opportunity to observe the topographic forms such as the river beds. It is therefore, obvious that under normal conditions, the river beds are filled with water that occupies and running over it[2]. However, we see the same erosion mechanism on rivers. Since the flow rate, quantities of sand and pebbles are essential elements causing erosion, we conclude the same process, but on a larger scale compared to the models studied.

1.1.2.3. The Divergent meanders

A study on the aerial photos shows that their evolution is fast enough in the river Forcados and the estuaries. They are slower in the middle of the delta. However, we used aerial photos to compare the different periods on three towns: Amassoma, Brass fig 1.6 (A, B)) in Bayelsa State and Buguma in Rivers State to study this evolution. The study was carried out using aerial photographs of 1971 and 1979 for Brass, and Buguma and 1961, 1971 and 1979 for Amassoma (Source: Ministry of Lands & survey Port Harcourt, River State).

The characteristic of meandering rivers like Forcados and Nun tend to expand their curves. During the dry season at low tide, one can observe that the concave banks were attacked and show abrupt collapse. The convex edges of the banks develop a very gentle slope with a large deposit of sand (sand bank) when the concave bank is affected by major bank erosion. It was observed that the rate of erosion of the concave bank is proportional

---

[1]   Fig 1.9-Mechanism of erosion from the river edge at Amassoma.

[2]   In the rainy season (during floods)

(equals) to the rate of widening of the sandbank. This increases the meanders and erosion in such zones of the rivers and creeks as the rambling of the sand bank is faster. This we observed at the environments of Amassoma (river Nun), Sagama (river Forcados) and Odi (river Nun) (Fig 1.5). The profile of the river bed at Amassoma showed much greater depths on the concave bank. It is the same on the edges with the largest course mass of water caused by the tendency of all the movements to continue from West to the East-West direction along the river.

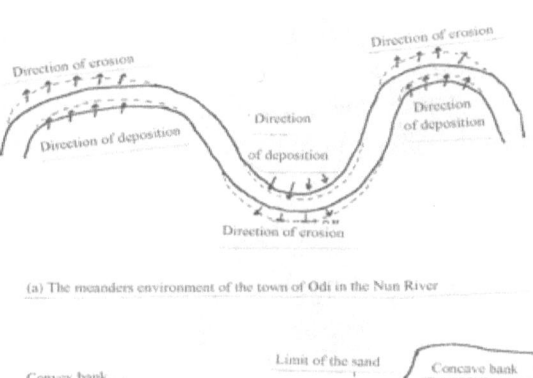

(a) The meanders environment of the town of Odi in the Nun River

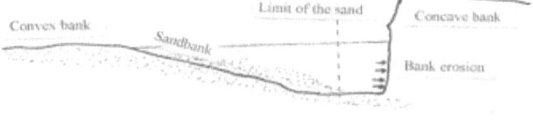
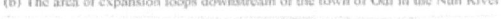

(b) The area of expansion loops downstream of the town of Odi in the Nun River

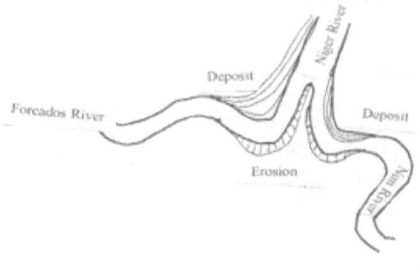

(c) The movement in the confluence of Forcados and Nun

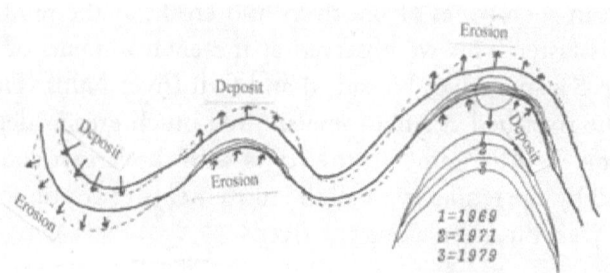

(d) Meanders at Amassoma.   (e) Evolution paths
(not to scale).

Fig 1.5: The displacement of the zone of meanders and loops. The arrows show the direction of movement of the meanders.

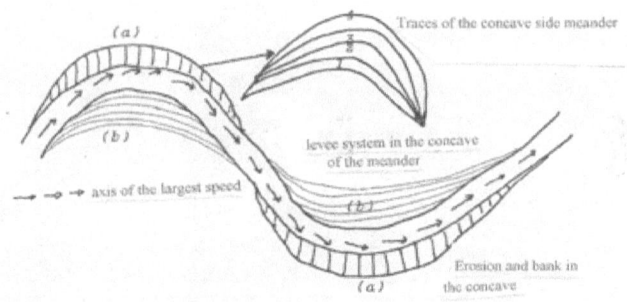

A: The River Banks and system of the levees.

We saw from the evolution of the erosion at Amassoma that the intervals of the traces are based on the flood, the flow rate and the volume per second for the same period in succession. Compare the paths of 1969, 1971 and 1979 in fig. 1.9 (e). Drawn from aerial photos (shown diagrammatically).

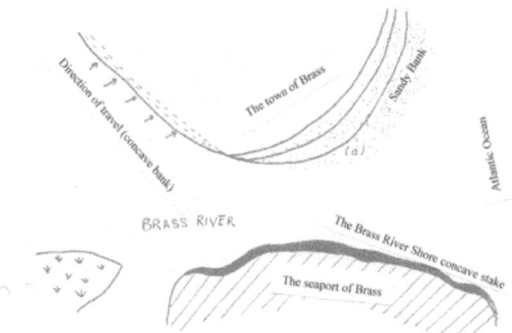

B: The situation at Brass is special case port (a) is filled up by dredging each year. However, the meandering courses of displacement cannot correspond to the normal tracings. This means an action that is not natural.

Fig 1.6: The general situations of River banks and system de levees/estuaries.

A comparable analysis of meanders on a map of 1/110000 of 1971 and the present states of Rivers Forcados, Niger and Nun shows that the zones of higher buckles are more meandering with the largest deposit of sand (Fig 1.8c). However, the expanding buckles have limitations, because they are sharpest between the bank of the concave bank and the limit of the sand bank (fig 1.8d) to the convex bank.

In the middle delta, the moving meanders are somewhat insignificant due to the period between the two aerial photos considered. However, there has been displacement in some rivers and tidal creeks, but that's not enough to draw a general conclusion to represent the movement of meanders in the delta. It needs at least, 25 years intervals in other to observe a significant shift of meanders[1] to represent a general conclusion to represent (movement of meanders) in the delta.

Anyway, in the absence of such a research, our partial conclusion could be valid as a general mechanism of the process of the movement.

---

[1]   The bottom of the river bed

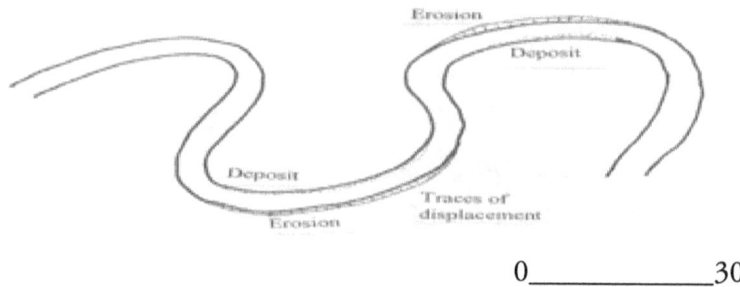

0_____30

(a) The movement of meanders (Buguma, Rivers State)

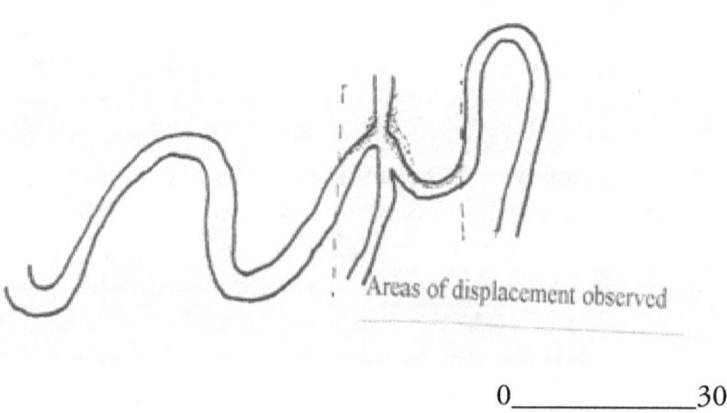

0_____30

(b) Movements in the confluence near Buguma, Rivers State.

Fig 1.7: The meanders in the middle delta.

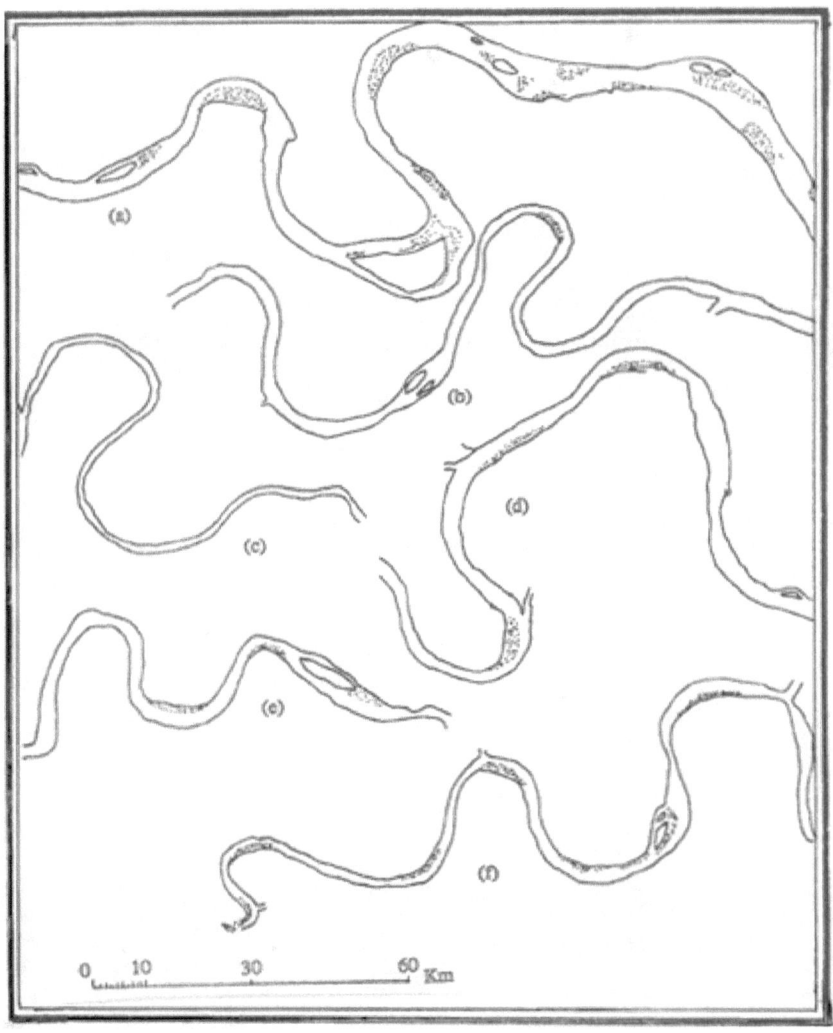

A: The types of meanders of Rivers Nun, Niger, Forcados and creeks in the upper delta. At (a) Odi, (b) Oweikorogha, (c) Seibokorogha, (d) Egbedi, (e) Oporoma, (f) Amassoma.

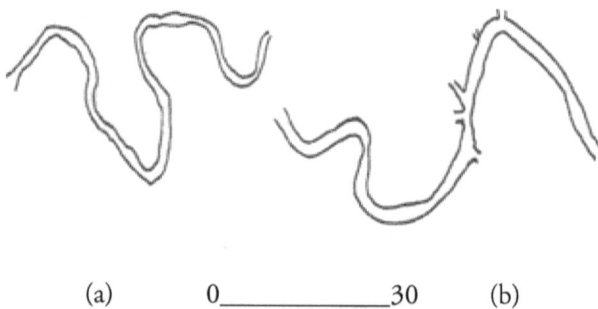

(a)   0_____30   (b)

(a) River Sombreiro between Obule I & II
(b) Buguma Creek between Ilelema & Sama

(c).River Orashi0_____30(d) Saka Creek

0_____30

(a).Surprise Creek (*Aguriki to Ljamikiri*)

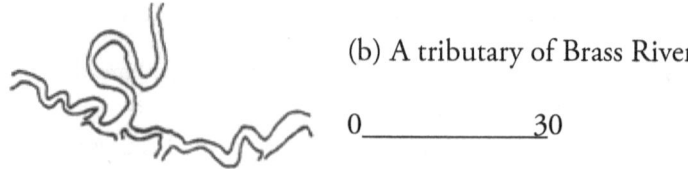

(b) A tributary of Brass River

0_____30

B—The meanders in the middle Delta

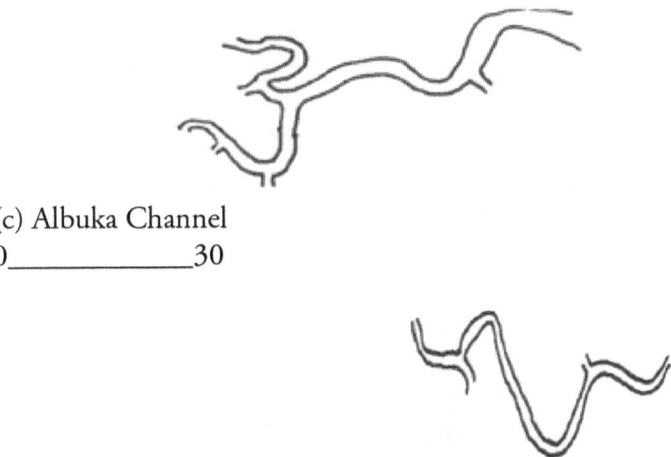

(c) Albuka Channel

0_____30

(d) Creek near Jekegbene

C: The meanders in the lower delta

Fig 1.8: The various types of meanders in the delta

The coastal Niger Delta seems to be a collection of multiples of such meanders given its form like a giant mesh.

The lower delta, like the upper delta has a displacement of the meanders observed in the period (1971-1979) (Fig 1.8). But human activities have put barriers in the direction of the movement; for example, construction of ports or shorelines (piling) at Brass, Bonny etc (fig 1.8). Under these conditions, backfilling the minor bed is much faster by filling and by erosion of the sandy bank (convex)[1]. This is most probably the reason why the port of Brass is backfilling faster than other ports in the delta[2].

1.1.2.4. The Kingdom of water

The Niger Delta is characterized by the existence of multiple rivers with numerous streams (various) meeting in a labyrinth of creeks, lagoons and islands of various sizes. The Niger Delta is like "an old unplanned city" where the wide rivers represents the highways (River Niger), other rivers

---

[1]   In the coastal shore.

[2]   The port is opens on to the Atlantic Ocean.

the streets, the streams and the creeks-the closes, etc, while the islands are the built up areas.

The Niger River and its tributaries are the only sources of water causing the flooding[1] with the local rains. These rivers sub-divide in the delta into other rivers such as Benin, Bonny etc. In fact, the Niger delta is composed of 14 well-defined rivers from West to east of the delta: rivers Benin, Escravos, Forcados, Ramos, Dodo, Fishtown, Sagana, Nun, Brass, Saint Nicholas, Santa Barbara, San Bartholoméo, Sombreiro et Bonny (fig 1.2). To these is added a multitude of creeks and other smaller rivers. Observation of aerial photographs shows that the Niger delta consists also of a multitude of Islands of which the rivers, creeks, streams, etc formed the cement that holds them together. One can also compare the delta to a labyrinth where the rivers, creeks and streams form the pedestrian streets. The Islands appear to be an oil stain when observed from above in an aircraft at low altitude with generally swamps in or at the interior of the Island (Wilberforce Island where Amassoma is situated).

However, the area occupied by water is greater than that occupied by the dry land. We estimated it to about two-thirds of the delta

1.2.0. The Mangroves.

The mangrove is the area where fresh water rivers and salt water of the Ocean mix to form brackish water. The soils are either, permanently submerged during the high tide (flood tide) and exposed at low tide (ebb-tide). However, soils have a high salinity.

The area of inter-tidal mangrove covers an area of 4921 km² from the coastline of 1139.6 km² of the delta, but Allen took about 8997.66 km². This difference is probably from the method used and the period (Dry or rainy seasons or the aerial photographs of the periods.) or surface area he covered.

The barrier beach Islands, cut by tidal channels mangroves separated the sheltered side (inner-part) of the beach islands from the Ocean. The mangroves area covers an area of 8 km² to 16 km². The tidal range is the difference between the lower level and the highest level of the tides.

In fact, low-lands and estuaries offer many common characteristics. The most common characteristic is that of the existence of channels cut by

---

[1]   Adding to the local rainfall in the delta.

tidal currents and areas of sedimentation. It may be that the origin of the marshes and estuaries is in the Flanders transgression that sent low-lying areas other than the river outlets[1] and estuaries. Deposits are made in the estuaries during the Transgression that slowed the river flow by decreasing the slope. The recent quaternary coastal Niger delta occupies a volume greater than 900 km².

The deposition of earth elements in suspension in the freshwater is more rapid in the transition zone. This is probably due to chemical actions whose explanation is more complex and requires special equipment. However, the simplest explanation we can give is that the presence of salt in the ocean water has probably caused the rapid sedimentation of the elements. The torpidity increases as we move away from that area toward the ocean at low tide. The swamps[2] are formed either by clogging in the sheltered side of the estuaries and is back by a protective barrier in the bay.

1.3.0. The Marshlands (Photo 1.2)

The marshlands (wetlands) are in the freshwater zone especially in the swampy plains between the curvet of Amassoma and the terrace of Sombreiro River, occupying 11,890,000 ha.

The lowlands are generally composed of amphibious trees such as raphia palm trees etc. Dry land seems to go, but they often give rise to swamps where the distance varies from few metres to hundreds or more.

---

[1]   The marshes

[2]   It should be noted that in the freshwater areas, swamps are formed at the rear of the rivers at a distance varying from 20 to 800 m or even more.

(a) Built in swampy area.

(b) North-west of the above area (a).

(c) Erosion caused by runoff (*net flow*);
(d) Runoff of precipitation (*rainfall*)
The two photos (c, d) show the formation of runoff Channels.

Photo 1.2: Swamps: Typical situation of towns along rivers Forcados and Nun etc.

1.4.0. The major problems of morphological Units.

1.4.1. Erosion

Erosion is a natural phenomenon that results in a transformation of the relief. This transformation can take the form of wear on the ground surface (Photo 1.2 (c, d)). There are many natural actions involved in the action of erosion. So we can give a challenge to erosion as the set of natural phenomena attack or processing relief or surface of the earth including the action of water (as part of our research). In the Coastal Niger Delta, the erosion is most important in the months of May to August on the river banks. That is from the beginning of the floods to early August.

The Coastal Niger Delta like any other marine delta is formed by the accumulation of sediments from the Niger River and it tributaries that cause erosion. However, the Niger delta is a flat region with low-lying flood plains. The changes in temperature and humidity cause expansion and contraction due to variations in the water content of the soil and thus determine their mechanical damage. The ground is exposed unavoidably to the action of atmospheric features erosive power, including the rain. Rain, when it falls and streams after its fall, moves and causes elements of the earth, causing their transportation.

We are concerned with two major forms of erosion in the Niger Delta that cause problems to the extension and developing towns in the delta: (a) The erosion by detachment of the constituents of the soil particles and drive by water runoff. (b) Landslides on the river banks.

1.4.1.1. Erosion by the detachment of the constituent particles of the soil.

This type of erosion affects all towns in the delta particularly during the rainy season. The components are detached by rainfall and runoff with a superficial drainage, relatively homogeneous in the space of water holding in suspension or towing the elements of the soil ripped (photo 1.2 c, d). The Soil particles are carried by the water from the rain following the small grooves forming on the un-built surface. In the general case, this phenomenon is caused by a flow of water from a stream of water concentration in the flow rate[1] and velocities are able to produce the erosive action (Photo 1.2 (a)). In most towns in the delta, the direction is towards the back of the town or city. That is towards the swamp, except town/city that located on the flood plains, but became high enough and above the flood level. In such towns, the flow direction is towards the river or creek or stream, while some flow into the swamp to the back of the town. This phenomenon is clearly observable by the presence of drains and ditches that are created on the urban tissues (Photo 1.2 (c, d)) it is serious if the direction of the runoff water from the rain heads to the river. Such case causes and accelerates the landslides. This type of landslide on the river bank causes the lost of large quantities of soil each year into the

---

[1]   Fig 1.9-Mechanism of erosion from the river edge at Amassoma.

[2]   In the rainy season (during floods)

rivers. This combination threatens the peoples who built their houses on the river banks (Photo 1.3).

1.4.1.2. The landslide on the river bank.

The phenomenon of landslides of the river bank is often caused by the infiltration of water from the surface or by horizontal seepage of underground water and when it encounters an impermeable level inside the ground, stops. The seepage of a large volume of water can establish at this level a supersaturated soil with water. That is a lubricated level. However, the mass of the elements that keep the slope disappears. Then the landslide occurs.

In fact, the phenomenon of detachment of the land is located on the banks of rivers, creeks, or streams or even lakes. The mechanism of separation as we have observed is given in fig.1.9.

Photo 1.3: A dwelling house affected by the phenomenon of erosion combined with runoff and landslides. A house, half carried away by landslides of the river bank during the rainy season (Amassoma1988).

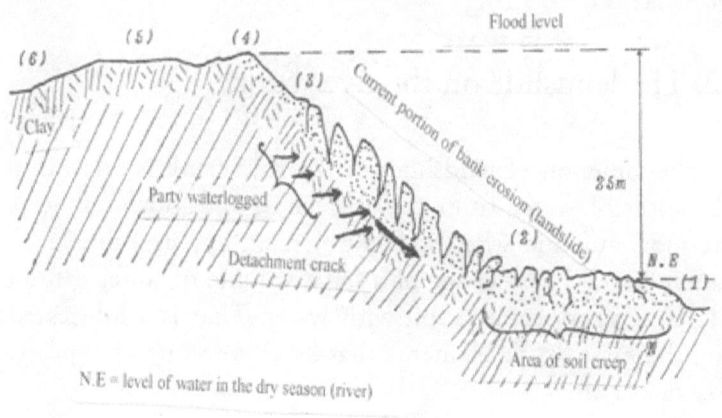

Fig 1.9: The mechanism of landslide at the river banks-a general case.

The same mechanism and characteristics were observed all along the rivers Forcados, Niger and Nun[1] but Table 1.2: below summarizes the general cases of erosions especially those caused by rainfall (runoff) and by the river (landslide).

Season	The Morphological Units					
	Bottom of the riverbed	Part of Banks (Lower)	Part of Banks (Upper)	Coastal Ridges	Basins (Draining)	Basin (Deep)
Dry December To March	(1) River Erosion	(2) Rain Erosion	(3) Rain Erosion /Water Gorges	(4) Rain Erosion (Runoff)	(5) Rain Erosion	(6) Rain Erosion

---

[1]   In the freshwater, because the phenomena and characteristics are different in the fresh water. However, erosion by runoff is the same mechanism and characteristic.

Rain April to July	River Erosion	Rain Erosion (Runoff)	Rain Erosion (Water Gorges)	Rain Erosion (Runoff)	Runoff Erosion	Runoff Erosion
Flood August to October	River Erosion	River Erosion	River Erosion	Rain Erosion (Runoff)	Agitation of water + Runoff, if not completely flooded.	

Table 1.2: Erosion cause by rainfall and surface runoff water.

1.5.0. The coastal morphology of the Niger Delta

View by air, the Niger delta seems to be a curve or a half moon. It consists of a chain of barrier islands, two types of sand ripples with a flat tidal land (fig 1.2) where the sediment settles to the coastal beach. That is the region which extends down to the alternating migratory movements which characterize the dynamic of the beaches of the Niger delta, as the Atlantic Ocean is particularly agitated at low tide.

The marshes behind the coast are characterized by the accumulation of mud in sheltered areas. This is the region where the shelter is reasonably well made so that the depths mediocre sandy deposits. Barrier beaches cover an area of 3,390,000 ha[1] while the unstable environment of the estuaries covers 1,380,000 ha.

The dynamics of the coastal morphology is determined by the current that built the well sorted sandy beach ridges ending with a gentle slope towards the Ocean and steep inward. Approximately 36 millions of water courses, marshes and flow channels, 61 at ebb tide into the small estuaries of Digatoru and 405 at that of Bonny, the largest.

---

[1]   Environ 12.14% of the Delta (East).

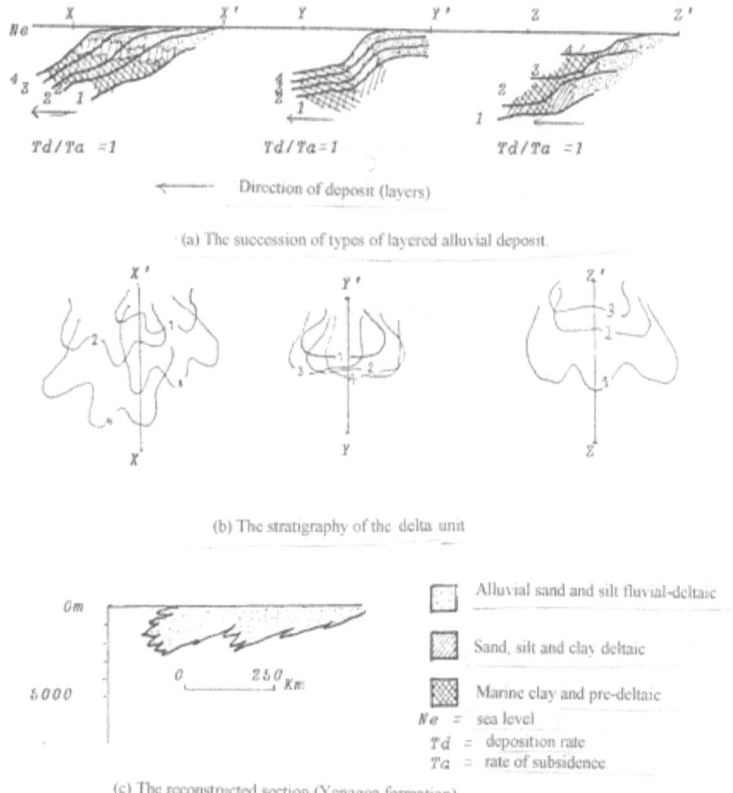

$Td/Ta = 1$ $Td/Ta = 1$ $Td/Ta = 1$

⟵ Direction of deposit (layers)

(a) The succession of types of layered alluvial deposit.

(b) The stratigraphy of the delta unit

0m

5.000

0   250 Km

Alluvial sand and silt fluvial-deltaic

Sand, silt and clay deltaic

Marine clay and pre-deltaic

Ne = sea level
Td = deposition rate
Ta = rate of subsidence

(c) The reconstructed section (Yenagoa formation)

The succession is sedentary and the framework expressed in terms of *deposition rate (Td) and rate of subsidence (Ta) in fig 24a. Td= Ta. That is the development of the deltaic unit is stationary, but the construction continues. Other regions fig 24c Tb>Ta shows a reconstruction.*

Consultation of various documents leads us to conclude that the local variations of Ta and Td give shape and distinct and different thickness of sedimentary and structural units. The special features of the estuaries of rivers

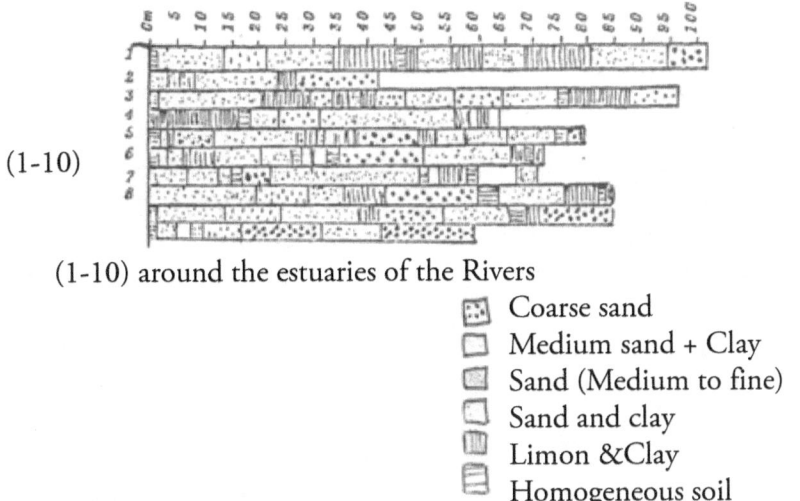

(1-10)

(1-10) around the estuaries of the Rivers

Coarse sand
Medium sand + Clay
Sand (Medium to fine)
Sand and clay
Limon &Clay
Homogeneous soil

(d). Layers encountered in drilling (Prepared according to Whitman)

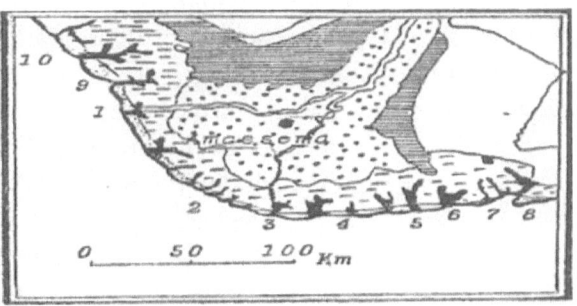

The Rivers: *(1) Forcados (2) Sagana (3) Nun (4) St Nicholas (5) St Bartholoméo (6) Sombreiro (7) Bonny (8) Andony (9) Dodo (10) Benin. Dry land + swamp = Qd; Alluvial plain environment (freshwater) = Continental Qfs & Qmb; Mangrove swamp; Beach and Barrier Island; estuaries; Qmb =Deposits in the regions of the meanders (1974); Qd = Deposit in the delta plain (1974); Qfs = Deposit in the fresh water and brackish water (1974); (e) The main sedimentary environments and the morphological structure of the complex of the Niger Delta today.*

Fig 1.10: The succession of the types of alluvial and sedimentary framework (A. Whitman 1982).

There is alluvial sand parallel to young hydro-orphic soils that extend to the ocean, depending on the contributions of successive floods. For example the regions of Elele and Bori have red literati soils with a secondary forest. Good agricultural land is rare in the delta except these regions.

Deposition in the barrier islands form part of the beach and coral (beach ridges) complexity of barrier islands which border the ocean to the limit 480 km (fig 1.10). The coral beaches and barrier islands continue west-wards to the environment of Lagos. The complex barrier islands consist of beaches and sand ridges that are developing in relation to old lines. There are 20 well defined barrier islands visible in the Niger Delta which are separated from others by deep channels variation of the tides[1]. The surface of these barrier islands is a few hundred metres to 12 km in width and length ranging from 4.80 to36.80 km and with an average of 17.6 km. Seen from the Ocean, the islands have straight edges, while the side of the inside edges are irregular and eroded caused by the tides (high and low) in the creeks[2]. The islands have a height of 2.75 m environ while the minimum average is 1.83 m and the maximum is 3.53 m[3].They are maintained by palm trees (coconuts), woody brushes, grasses and a high atmospheric humidity on the surface.

The variation of the horizontal distance between high and low tides marks a length of 30.48 m while the average minimum is 15.24 m and the maximum is 45.72 m. The slopes are about 1% to 0.50%[4], while in the slopes in the eroded areas appear to be higher 1:5 to 1:10.

---

[1]   High and low tides in the deep channels that separate the barrier islands.

[2]   Are meandering creeks. Causing erosion on the coast forming the convex barrier islands.

[3]   Estimates, for we do not have the necessary instrument to give an exact dimensions.

[4]   An average of 1 in 100 to 1 in 500.

Chapter 2

The Floods

The coastal Niger delta is confronted with flooding, especially during the rainy season. This is an increase in volume of water in the rivers, creeks and towns/villages, but the river Niger remains the main cause of the floods overflowing the rivers.

2.1.0. The origin of the flooding of the delta.

The Niger River and its tributaries are the principal causes of the flooding in the Niger delta. The river Niger takes its source 800 m above sea level on the northern slope of the dorsal Guinean (fig 2.1) from where it flows over 250 km to the north-east. It spreads in the vast alluvial plain of the Inland Niger Delta of 30.000 sq km in Macina (Prof. Gallais 1967) after passing a series of rapids at Sotuba. At this level, they inter-mingled in the base of distributor lakes; swamps that cover the high waters[1] and receive from River Bani[2] at the confluence of Mopti. The slope between Mopti and Niafounké is 20 mm per kilometre.

The river bed changes direction to south-west to north-east to the city of Timbuktu, then turns sharply to east by capture at Gao[4] and meets the old course to the east of the Niger River.

---

[1]   The slope between Mopti and Niafounké is 20 mm per kilometre.

[2]   One of the main tributaries is 298 m above sea level and 2,500 km from the sea.

[3]   The great valley of Tilemsi

[4]   Study site for the construction of a dam.

The downstream of the Inland Niger delta is divided by rapids in succession at Ansongo, Labobezenga (western Niger) which meanders adjudicate the quartzite Atkora[1], Yelwa and Bussa (Nigeria). It is from Bussa that the Niger River receives from the permanent tributaries, including the larger Kaduna which descents from the Jos plateau, Benue coming from the Adamawa massive, a navigable river from the Cameroon.

---

[1]   The great valley of Tilemsi

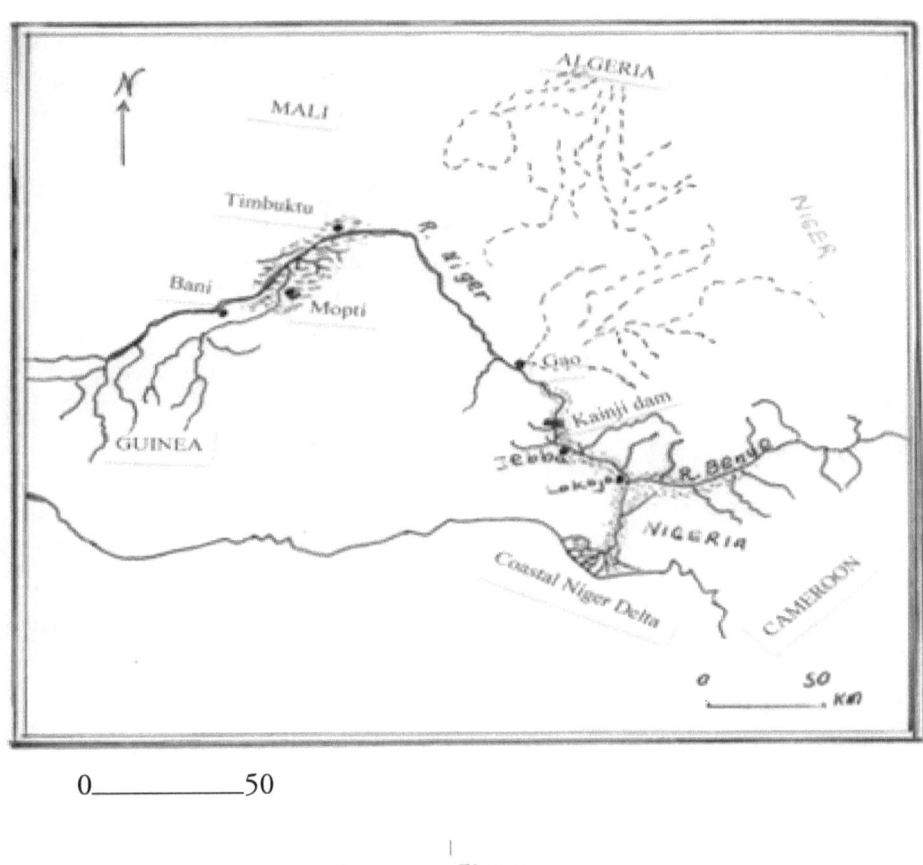

0_____50

———	Watercourse
- - - -	Rivers seasonality
⅏	Rapid
▦	Floodplain
▨	Floodplain

Fig 2.1: The course of the Niger River and its tributaries.

2.2.0. From the Niger River and its tributaries

The flooding of the Niger River, before arriving at the Coastal Niger delta passes through at least two seasons in it source from the dorsal Guinea. In fact, in the upper part of the Niger River, the flood is simple.

The rainy season in Guinea commerce in April; and May at Bamako (fig 3.1). This is during the beginning of the floods in June, the flow is contrasted at Sotuba for example the mean flow is 54 m3 per second while in the high waters the average is of 6,200 m3 per second. Water spreads out slowly in the lakes at the distributaries (Macina) where the flood is delayed until December at Timbuktu, at Niamey (Republic of Niger) in February and the flood takes place at Gao in the dry season. Indeed until the beginning of the next season, the Niger River is feed only by its local tributaries. Subsequently, joins the floods from the Benue River, one of its major tributaries, which doubles the floods, swelling the river Niger in February. March is the month to which the flood[1] reaches the upper Niger.

2.3.0. Local Rainfall

The local rainfall also contributes to the rising flood of the Coastal Niger delta. The rains began in the Niger Delta in late March until mid-October. Indeed, the very heavy Rainfalls are concentrated on few months (in the year): In June, July and September with a decline in August[2].

These rains result in an increase in volume of flooding of the rivers, creeks, swamps and floodplains causing the overflow of lowlands (plains).

It is therefore obvious that these two phenomena: (a) the flooding of the Niger River and its tributaries and (b) local precipitations (rainfall) are the root causes of flooding in the Coastal Niger Delta.

2.4.0. The hydrology of the Niger Delta.

The Niger delta is a lowland region with a channel system of natural waters in which the Niger River enters and crosses to the Atlantic Ocean. The groundwater level of the entire Niger Delta does not exceed 45.70

---

[1]   In the following year from the beginning of the rainy season and flooding the upper Niger River

[2]   Is popularly known as 'the August break' which is almost disappearing may be due to climatic changes.

m above the ground (Nedeco 1961 and Dangan 1981). The region has a small slope, average elevation of less than 8 m. The hydrology of the basin is a river type drained to the Atlantic Ocean.

2.4.1. The regime of rivers adductor

The Niger River is still the main source of water in the Niger delta, with unique channel. Two other streams on the limits of flood plains are located on the east and west of the Niger River. The low flood plain is wider with a gentle slope. The Niger River at this level is divided into several major meander tributaries.

The two branches of the Niger River in its lower level are the rivers Forcados and Nun, but other rivers and streams unite in a various labyrinths of creeks and lagoons. The distribution of water from river Niger into the two branches is uneven. The Forcados has the largest volume of water (59%) and Nun (41%). The distributing channels are flanked by low levees descending to the swamps forest.

The regimes of the rivers in the Niger Delta depend on the regime of the Niger River (graph 2.1) and sea water. However, it is worth thinking about the seasonal variations in water volume, especially the Niger River, if we have to search for solution on the problems on floods and flooding on the extending, planning and developing the towns in the delta.

The River Niger, with a length of 4,160 km crosses almost all the climatic zones of West Africa, ie the rainy season in semi-desert and still rainy season. It takes its source in an area of very heavy rainfall[1] where it joined the rivers Niantan, Milo and Tinkiso in addition to this volume of rainfall in South of Mali. The floods reach their peak levels in May/June on the upper and heads to Mali "semi-desert" Here, the waters extend to the Inland Niger delta of the Niger River and delayed until December to Timbuktu. Most of the floods are lost by evaporation and irrigation in the Inner Niger delta. The rest continues on its way to the Republic of Niger in February during the peak of the dry season[2].

Arriving in Nigeria, the Niger River meets rainy season, a country were the precipitation is comparably high adding to the local precipitations and

---

[1]   The Guinea.

[2]   This means a blessing for farmers for irrigation with a slight increase in volume during the floods in the rainy season. The Niger River has a varied regime.

its tributaries such as the Benue river increasing the volume of the River water. The maximum height is attained between August and October at Jebba . . .the Flooding from Guinea arrives in Nigeria the following year (a year later).

As a result, Niger is at its lowest level in April-June-July, in Nigeria where the local precipitation increases again.

The two branches of the Niger River (Forcados and Nun) and their tributaries have the same regime affected by high tides and low tides with an increase in volume during the floods in the rainy season. The Niger River has a varied regime. The two branches of the Niger River (Forcados and Nun) and their tributaries have the same regime affected by high tides and low tides.

2.5. The Floods and flooding.

We mean by floods in the delta, the overflow waters that cover the low plains, cities, towns etc. They are caused by periodic flooding of the Niger River, its tributaries and local rainfall. The exceptional floods in the delta are due to rain showers and prolonged intense rains. They are aggravated by the combination of floods from various tributaries, including the Niger River and it tributaries from dorsal Guinea. The problem of flooding in the Niger delta can be analysed in two words: rainfall and flooding. However, we chose two stations to record the rainfall. They are Amassoma and Brass[1].

The floods are strong and undermined the banks, forming steep of up to 25 m high above the low water level. Flood flows are distributed at a volume percentage of 59% (Forcados) and 41% (Nun).

2.5.1 The freshwater zone (graph 2.2).

The zone covers an area of 9,750,000 ha. Is an area of low alluvial flood plain of the Niger River and splits into flood plain and it extends to the ocean which depends on the contribution of successive floods of the Niger River. Indeed, this area also has many sources that cause flooding:

---

[1]   Amassoma (fresh water zone) located in the central delta and Brass located at the coast (brackish water zone)

flood, swamp and human activities. The increase of floods began at the end of April, the month that marks the beginning of the rainy season. Initially, the daily increase is about 2 to 5 mm on the average until the end of May[1]. The months of June, July marks an increase in the daily average to about 5 to 8 mm, due to the arrival of the floods, and precipitation from the interior of the Niger River. The highest increase recorded was in September. However, the minimum varies from 30 to 60 mm, while the maximum varies from 50 to 90 mm. In September[2] we also observed a significant decrease that goes down sometimes up to 5 mm in 24 hours, but does not in anyway a recession.

In fact, the Coastal Niger delta is highly influenced by the micro-climate due to humidity (atmospheric) local rainfall. There are two phenomena in the period: if a heavy rain spreads over greater part of a given area, for example Amassoma and its environment within a radius of 5 km, this will result in a significant increase in the flood. As against a shower of equivalence, but localized at Amassoma will not significantly increase the flood level. And there were days we observed a significant decrease on the water level with the average atmospheric temperatures of 24°C at 9h30; 36°C at 13h30 and 27°C at 17h30 (average temperatures we recorded from 15th August to 30th September).

---

[1]   From one of our stations located at Aya-Ogbo-ama (Amassoma).

[2]   Same phenomenon in October.

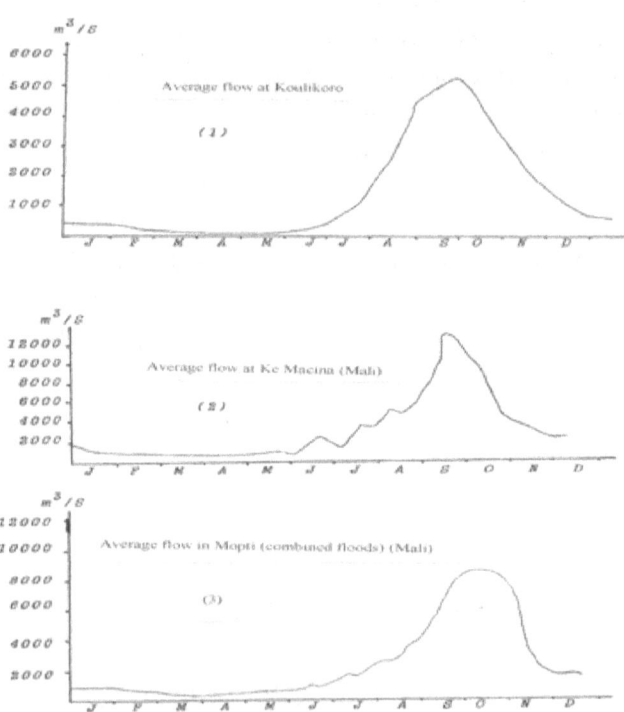

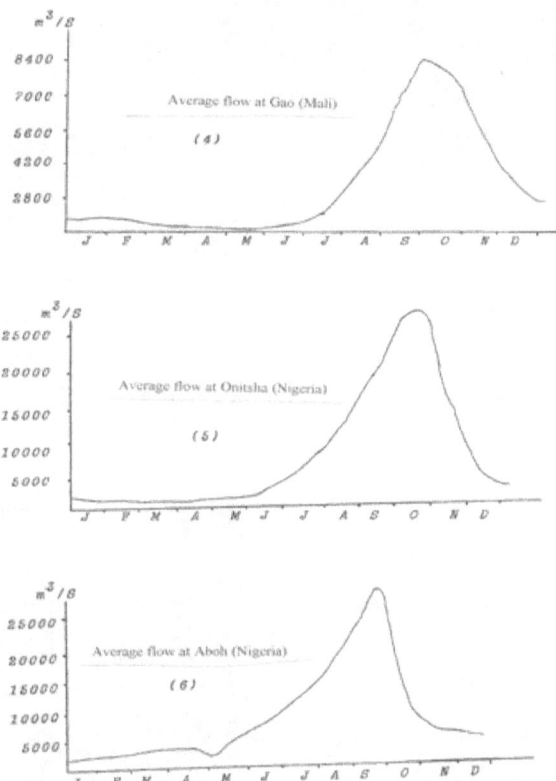

Graph 2.1: The average monthly flow of various points of the river Niger (1979)

(a) A house built to avoid flooding. Note the height of the DPC (red floor) 1.2 m on the side of the stairs. Amassoma 1988.

(b) A house invaded by the floods Amassoma.

Photo 2.1: The floods.

(a) The layout of the flood level (Yenagoa 1988)

(b) The height of the flood level (Amassoma 1988).

Photo 2.2: The levels of flooding (1988)

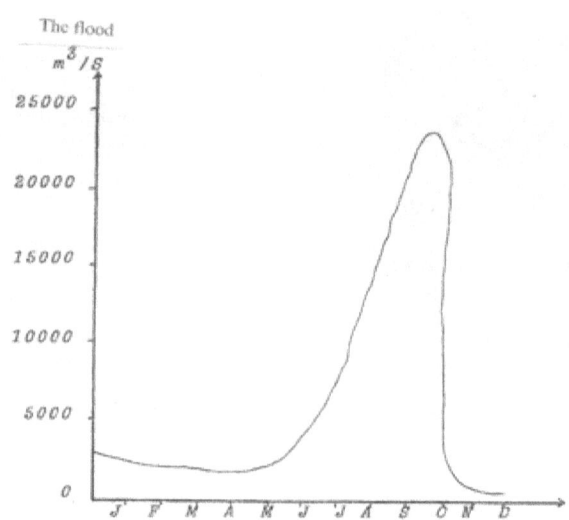

(a) The daily average flow of River Niger at Onitsha (on 37-years of observation NEDECO)

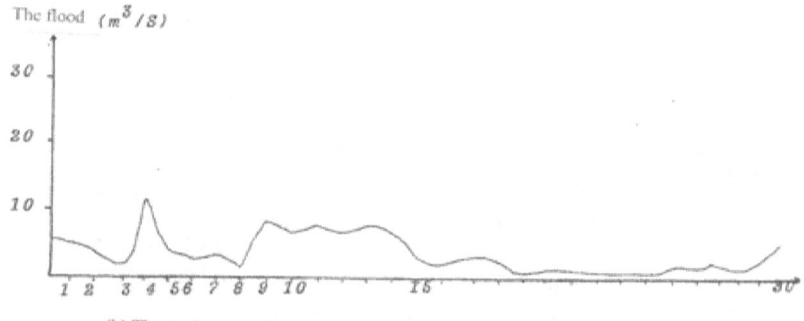

(b) The evolution of the daily flooding at Amassoma, recorded in September 1989

Graph 2.2: The evolution of daily floods and flow rates.

(a) Photo taken during a 2 hours heavy rainfall (Amassoma).

(b) Municipal market invaded by floods (Yenagoa)

Photo 2.3: Floods and its disadvantages.

Since the rivers are empting into the Atlantic Ocean at the Gulf of Guinea, these slight changes may be quite possible (a drop of floods).

The rate of increase in volume of the rise in flooding of the river Forcados is slightly higher than that of river Nun. It is however, from 3 to 5 mm (average) above those of Nun River. Flooding from swamps in certain areas or towns (Amassoma, Yenagoa, Peremobiri, Otuan, Sagbama etc) are much faster and more disastrous than those of floods from the rivers except the River overflows its banks through the town. Almost all of these towns are on the edge of rivers and tributaries, but in front of swamps[1] except at Sagbama[2] behind a flood plain. These swamps are easily flooded by the least rainfall. Moreover, in some parts of swamps and marshes, the water is collected throughout the year. However, during the rainy season, the volume of water collected in the marshes increases. Since the slope is down towards the rear of the town, the floods spread to the towns, aggravated by human factors.

The human factor is one of the major ways that people use for fishing shrimps. It consists of digging a channel[3] from the bank of the river to the swamps. Thus, before the rivers overflow its banks, water is already flowing into the rear of the town or swamps and adds to the water already collected in it. Other human interventions are the elements for the construction of the traditional homes and fills (borrow pits) to elevate (raise) the ground floor above the flooding levels (variations) (photo 2.1 (a), 2.2 (b)).

The duration of flooding is determined by the site of the town. If the ground level is low, as in the cases of Peremabiri, Patani, Oporoma etc. Duration is about two months on the average. While at Amassoma, Yenagoa, Odi, it lasts about a month on the average. But in general the average duration of floods in the eastern part of the delta, specifically in the area of fresh water varies from one month to three months. This is the case in the towns, but in the case of flood plains, it varies from two to four months (average). The flood in the transition zone, are of marine origin and at high tide waterways due to the flooding of the river Niger, Nun[4], seem a meeting of two opposition fluvial and marine forces. These tidal forces and those of water flow of rivers Forcados and Nun.

During the rainy season, rivers Forcados and Nun have a unidirectional discharge toward the ocean (south). Indeed, the tide starts rising up into the estuaries with a force that changes the normal direction of flow at low tide.

---

[1] The town is often on the edge of the natural levees of rivers and at the rear of the towns is the swamp, that is to say: the river—the town—the swamp.

[2] As is the town of Amassoma.

[3] Up to 1 m depth and 1 m wide at the starting in the first years of creation.

[4] River observed and studied.

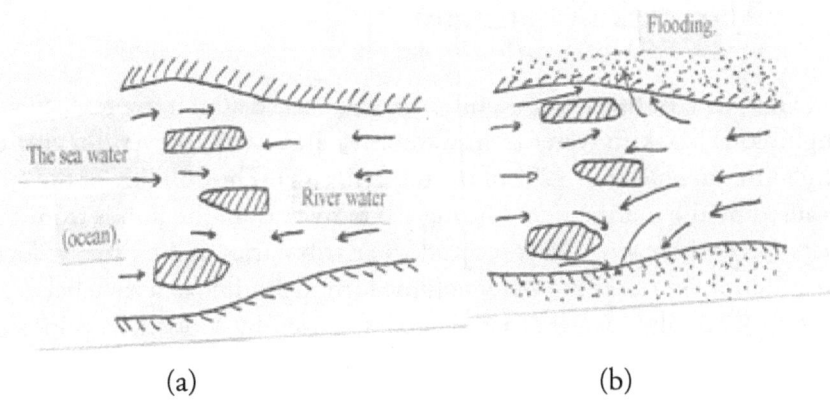

| (a) | (b) |

Sea Water   Fluvial (Water) Floods-

(a) meets the pressure of seawater at
    High tide and floods (from rivers)

(b) The waters of the ocean at high tide pushing the river
    Water, causing the overflow of the banks on both sides of
    the rivers and creeks

Fig 2.2: The phenomena of the flood and tide in the transition zone.

This force acts on the entire volume and the length of the zone of brackish water between the ocean and the transition zone[1]. On arrival at its lower level, meets the flow forces from the rivers and their tributaries. Since the strength of the marine tide is higher than that of the rivers, it tends to make this zone a "temporary death zone"[2]. This occurs from the lower limits of the transition zone and throughout the lower[3] Forcados and Nun rivers. So the transition zone acts as a temporary dam, causing daily flooding (fig 2.2) in the immediate environment and, beyond: such as at Olugbobiri, Peremabiri etc.

---

[1]   The transition zone. Zone where mixture of waters take place: fresh and salt waters.

[2]   A time that there is no flow of water in either direction. Acting like a lake.

[3]   The basins.

2.6.0. The Brackish water area.

This area is the largest unit in the Niger delta. It represents the amphibious brackish water (saline swamps) area, which covers an area of 12.05 million ha, about 42% of the total (fig 1.3). The flooding of the area is caused by the marine tide. During the rainy season, the floods from the rivers Niger, Forcados, Nun etc and their tributaries adding to the local precipitation increases the water volume forming buffer area zone between the fresh and saline waters that are characterized by sudden eruptions of fresh water in brackish water during the floods. This gives a corresponding increase in the level variations[1] high tide and low tide.

We notice weekly alternating very high tide variations at Buguma during the rainy season. That is a week of very high tide going above its banks that flooded habitations in the plains, beyond the normal tidal levels during a week; then follows a normal low tide the following week that does not go beyond its banks. This continues throughout almost the rainy season (July to September)

Although, this seems to be a common phenomenon in the brackish water zone, there are variations of the increasing levels of the tide and the flooding. That is a week of high tide and a small tide the following week. However, flood plains are easily identified by a mere observation on the grass on the floodplains.

---

[1] An increase in the level of the low tide and high tide compared to the levels in the dry season.

Chapter 3

The Climate

The climatic conditions of the coastal Niger Delta are controlled by two masses atmospheric air (fig 3.1) on the lower level: The Equatorial (marine) wind from South-West and the Tropical Continental winds from North-East (Harmattan).

As these two air masses are of tropical origin, the temperatures are high through out the year and the variation of temperature is only affected by the difference of relative humidity-specific air masses. The contact between these two air masses is called "*the Inter-tropical discontinuity*" by Walker[1]. Seasonal changes in climate are due to movement of this discontinuity to the North and South.

The average temperature is 27°C, the maximum is attained in February and March (graph 3.1), a period that marks the end of the dry season and the influence of the harmattan[2]. The months of July, August and September are the months most cloudy and at lower temperatures.

---

[1]   H. D. Walker: the monsoon in West Africa.

[2]   The harmattan gives a lot of heat during the day and cold at night.

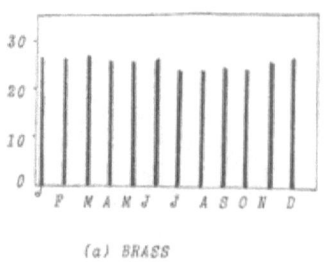

(a) BRASS

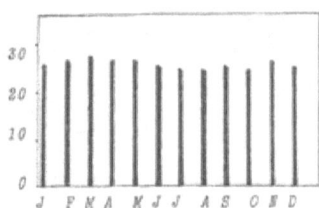

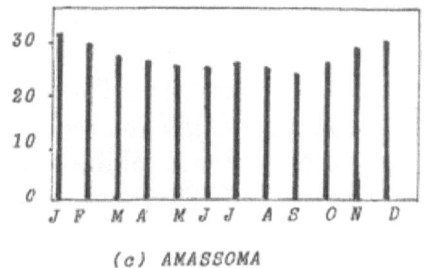

(c) AMASSOMA

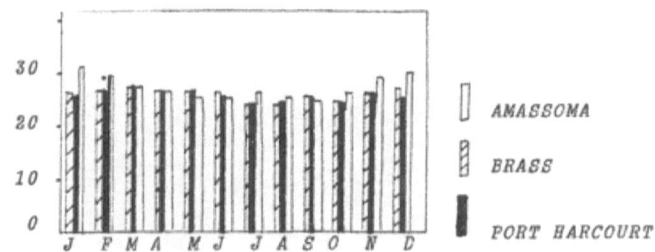

Graph 3.1: Average annual temperatures in the delta

The modification of temperature by altitude is not known in the Niger delta as it presents a low relief (maximum average altitude is within 20 m).

3.1.0. The Rains.

The rainfall in the Niger Delta is controlled by the mass movement of air from the north and south and the pressure zone (Graph 3.1). The minimum rainfall is in January. Each zone receives no more than 50 mm, except the coastal zone (Bonny, Brass, Akassa etc which has more than 50 mm (as in February). The minimum precipitation is 200 mm in march the month of July marks the arrival of the" monsoon from West Africa" in the coastal areas (fig 3.1). There is a decline in August, with a maximum in June-July-September (Graph 3.2).

Fig 3.1 shows a gradual decrease in rainfall from the coast to the interior: 4500 mm of rain, but a decrease of about 15 to 30 mm per kilometre. The months of less than 50 mm of rain last less than a month in the coastal area, it then increases gradually towards the interior of the delta. The number of rainy days[1] shows a distribution similar to the amount of rain per year. The absolute maximum data recorded indicates a heavy rain 200 mm per day in September and June. The maximum average most humid day reach 125 mm in the rainy season.

---

[1]   More than 1 mm of rain.

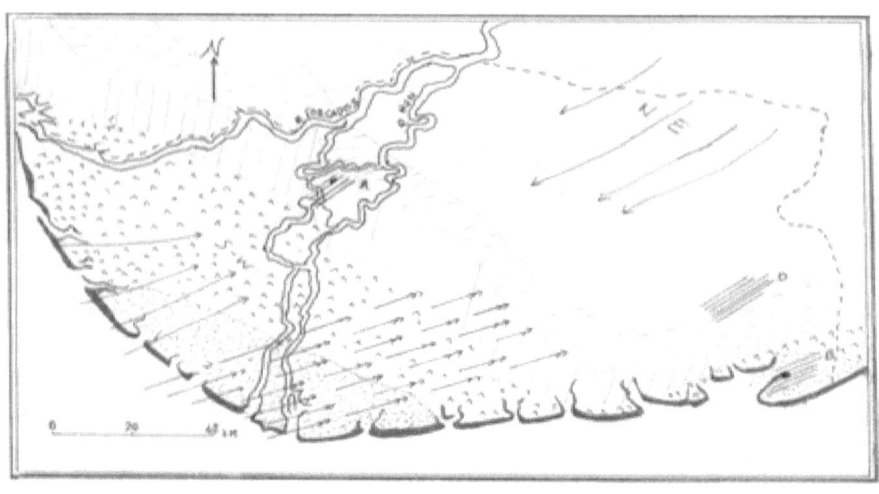

Average annual rainfall
- ☐ 2250-2500
- ▨ 2500-3000
- ▥ 3000-3500
- ▩ 3500-4000
- ▨ + 4000
- North-West wind (Marine wind)
- North-East wind (The harmattan)
- The tempest of 1989 (The area that was affected)
- Other areas: Amassoma (1965), Okrika (1975), Bonny (1980)

Fig 3.1: The climatic conditions of the delta.

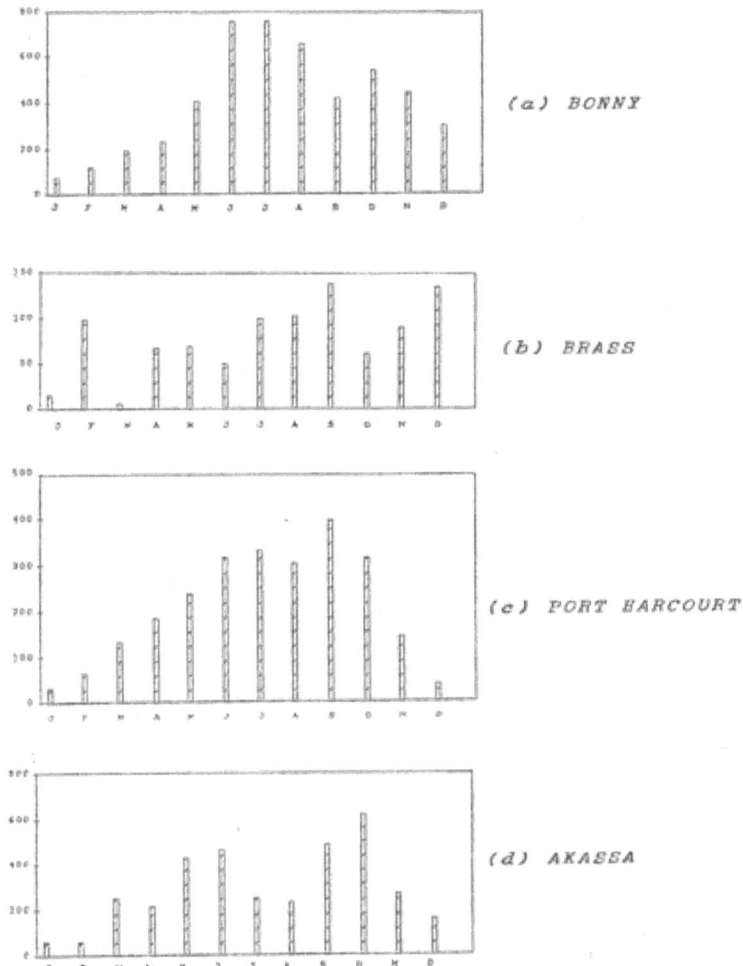

(a) BONNY

(b) BRASS

(c) PORT HARCOURT

(d) AKASSA

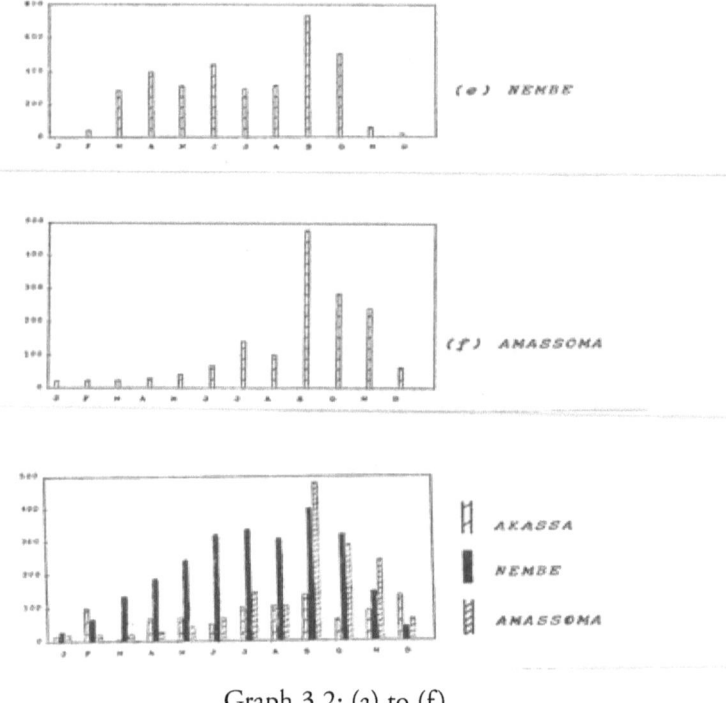

Graph 3.2: (a) to (f).

Graph 3.2: Comparative: The annual precipitation of a coastal town (Akassa), a town between 60 to150 km from the coast (Nembe), and a town in the central part of the delta (Amassoma). The graphic also shows the effects of micro-climate (Akassa and Amassoma). Also see Graphic 3.1.

3.1.1. The types of rain.

As the Niger delta is located in a tropical monsoon climate, the type of rain is conventional and often accompanied by thunder and lightening. Storms occur in the afternoon especially during the rainy season. The cause of such rainfall is most likely due to the rapid expansion and contraction of air masses caused by the temperature variations. For example, at our observation station at Amassoma, we observed several sunny days in September and October with an average recorded temperature of 36°C in the morning[1] and early afternoon. This period was often followed by a rain storm[2] about 12 hours, during the rainy season and early dry season and each change of tide was accompanied by a rain storm.

3.1.2. Relative Humidity

No air is completely dry, except some above tropical deserts, which contain very little water vapour, is this amount of water vapour we called humidity. But it is very important to know the relationship between the amount of water vapour and the actual amount of water vapour the air can hold at a given temperature. This report is the *"relative humidity"*. However, if we say that the relative humidity is 95% at 27°C (4), this means that the air retained 9.5 tenth of steam, it is possible to retain at 27°C. Saturated air is one that absorbs no more water vapour. That is, the relative humidity is 100%.

In the Niger delta, the relative humidity (all the year round) is about 95% to 100%, while the average ranges from 70% to 80%. It is higher near the coast and decreases towards the interior of the delta. It can significantly reduce in the day when the wind of harmattan blows, but the dry air descends only rarely to the coast.

3.1.3. The season of the Niger delta.

We define the seasons in the Coastal Niger Delta, the times of the year characterized by the presence of certain weather conditions such as rains, flooding and the state of the vegetation in particular during the dry season and just after the flood recession. There are two main seasons: the rainy season which begins from April to mid-October[3] and the dry season from mid-October to March ending.

---

[1]   Between 9:00 am and 12:30 pm

[2]   A heavy rain accompanied by thunder and lightening.

[3]   Cases of Amassoma and Yenagoa.

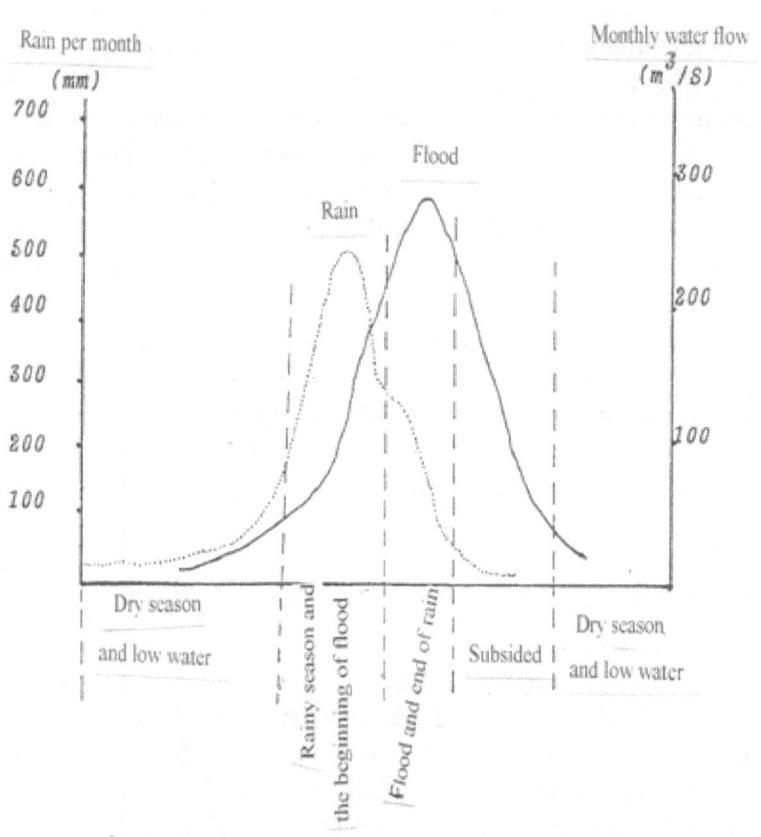

Graph 3.3: The Seasons of the Niger Delta

Summary of the Chapters

The Niger Delta is a developing region with development potentials and of a rapid economic development. So a rational management requires more and must be based on knowledge of the various geo-Eco-dynamic systems.

In fact, the Niger Delta consists of a multitude of rivers, creeks, channels, flood plains, marshes, swamps and mangroves and is dominated by water. In other words, the Niger delta is characterized by the existence of several rivers meeting in a labyrinth of creeks and lagoons. However, the successive governments privileged or prefers concentrating all developments projects around the capitals (in the delta): Port Harcourt (Rivers State), Yenagoa (Bayelsa State) etc.

Therefore, the morphology/topography has been an obstacle to expansion of the towns in the Niger delta. The delta further, is like a reservoir which collects the waters of the Niger River, its tributaries and the tributaries from its source at the dorsal Guinea, Benue River etc; thereby increasing the flooding of the rivers and towns in the delta causing the overflow.

The climatic conditions in the delta are controlled by two air masses, especially atmospheric and maritime equatorial South-Westerly wind and continental tropical-North-East or harmattan. The Coastal Niger delta is affected by the micro-climate which makes a considerable difference in rainfall. The maximum rainfall is in June-July and September.

The variation of which, the land is submerged is from a period of one to three months. The maximum relative humidity for the whole year is about 95% to 100%, but the average ranges from 70% to 80%.

It is therefore obvious that such an environment where water, creeks, rivers, marshes, swamps, floodplains and mangroves dominate (with lowlands) will eventually presents constraints to planning, development and extension of the delta towns, but is not impossibility.

This brings us to the analysis of urban solutions in the next chapters.

URBAN SOLUTIONS

We have in the previous chapters analysed the constraints of the delta environments, in particular, the coastal Niger Delta. These are topographical, morphological and others in particular the flood, climate etc. We will examine next in the following chapters the development and planning solutions under four chapters viz the water hazards (risks), types of cities and towns according to the morphologies of their locations (sites), public utilities, and the strategies of the Government's urban developing and planning efforts and programs in the delta.

Given the importance of Petroleum activities and oil fields, it is difficult to exclude the risk that these activities can pose to the environment of the Niger delta. This we will discuss in chapter one. In fact, there are several development, planning and extension projects in the delta towns or cities. Few of these projects were completed, many were abandoned either by the contractor, on the way or abandoned following a change of government.

The policy of the government on improving the living environment and health in the rural areas was initiated and pursued by all government authorities, since the down of independence, especially after the creation of states in the Niger delta: Rivers State and then Bayelsa State, which was carved out of Rivers State. People (the Government) have received consideration in this regard of development of rural areas. Though the Niger delta consists of towns of over 25,000 habitants, even metropolitan areas[1], it is still considered as a whole a rural area.

In Nigeria today, one of the problems of development and extension of towns and cities is that some continue to grow rapidly and others very slow and non homogeneous, some are relatively modern, while other areas remain rural and far lacking, such is the case of the Niger delta even though the country's economy depends on this region. The solution is to abbreviate the difference in the development processes and policies at the national (Federal) and local (States) levels and provide the means necessary to correct the bias and the non-homogeneity the regions (States) in an economy of space.

---

[1]   Port Harcourt, Warri, Sapele etc.

However, the problems of expansion[1] of towns in the Niger delta are quite different, particularly to those of other regions (States) in the country. These include morphological and topographical constraints. It is therefore clear that a general development plan for the entire country or States without taking into account the particularities of the regions (the Niger delta for example) will definitely be a failure, then what are these particular solutions for the Niger delta?

---

[1]   Development and planning.

Chapter 4

Water hazards

4.1.0. The weather and natural hazards

The low coastal areas of the Niger delta are not immune to marine disasters, as some more common phenomena of temporary elevations in the sea level as a result of exceptional meteorological events causing extensive material damage and that of human accidents.

The climatic conditions of the delta are controlled by two masses atmospheric at the lower level: the equatorial maritime winds of South-West and the tropical-continental North-East wind. These two air masses sometimes create strong winds influx of coastal waters and low atmospheric pressures that generate short-term increases in the sea level. However, the association of these phenomena in the tides result in a sudden acceleration of the kinetic energy of the coast, which is a risk of destruction and flooding of some coastal towns and villages, including the towns of Brass, Bonny etc.

The temporary increases in sea level as a result of weather agents are due to the confrontation of the equatorial maritime air masses of South-West and tropical-continental North-East. These are the leading low pressure systems, often very active. The characteristic of these systems is a strong pressure gradient that generates both strong winds and atmospheric pressure at sea level, very low. The position and orientation of the low sandy coast of the delta and the atmospheric circulation during extreme weather conditions are particularly important.

The combination of sea tide, of spring tide and the wind blowing South-West with a velocity of over 140 km/h in wind gusts associated with low atmospheric pressure appears to cause the total level flush waves leading to important materials degradation. Indeed, an isolated thunderstorm has caused a very large damage in the South-West of the coast (Brass, Akassa (fig 3.1)) during the night of 24th August 1989. The damages were caused by a sudden development of very strong winds from the Atlantic Ocean. The destruction was localized in a very wide corridor and oriented South-West/North-East. It crossed the islands of residence (town and villages) and mangroves. Houses most affected were the traditional houses and those built on wooden pillars. Some dwelling homes were completely destroyed; roofs were twisted or removed etc.

At Brass in the popular area (indigenous) where traditional houses outnumber (*part of this district which borders the river Brass*) about one third were destroyed and the roofs of some modern houses or semi-modern were pulled out. But in the fishing villages (*where most of the houses are made of thatches-fishing camps*), damages were more dramatic, because it was not only the roof and the house that was destroyed, but the whole house that was torn off to distances that varied from 50 to 200 m (*the variation of the distance depends on the distance from main camp*).

The local market of Akassa was also destroyed. Trees were uprooted or broken. Twisted tree trunks or near the break elated, were various debris thrown at great distances, including some caravanned of oil Companies (Agip, Shell etc) that had their roofs blown off from inside. These swirling phenomena are common in the Niger delta at this period of the year[1], but should not be confused with the ordinary storms or strong horizontal winds. They can also break trees, but the damage is punctual and not in a concentrated well defined corridor. In fact, all these phenomena lead to destruction of property of the towns and villages, also to erosion and coastal flooding in the Niger delta. The intensity of erosion and coastal degradation depends on the frequency and type of storms. But the authorities do not attach much importance to this subject.

Indeed, predictions of these phenomena including maritime on the coastal environment of the delta can only be analysed from historical data. As well as improving weather forecasting for long periods and establishment of experimental stations measure the hydrodynamic parameters. Unfortunately, modern measuring devices of these parameters are not available. In addition, measurements with the devices available are

---

[1]   Between the months of August and early October, just before the recession.

not done regularly, so such data are incomplete to be used for any reliable prevision and analysis yet.

4.2.0. The hydrological regime and maritime risks

The regime is at risk due to maritime water logging caused by the tides and floods during the inundations: for example the washing of lower exchangeable bases. The products in solution arrive at the shallow aquifers by infiltration directly or indirectly through the surface waters that communicate with them.

4.2.1. Maritime and Fluvial pollutions

Pollution is the infection of a natural environment by contaminants that cause instability, disorder, harm or discomfort to the <u>biological environment</u> (eco-system) that consists all the <u>organisms</u> living and nonliving (a-biotic) including physical components of the environment with which the organisms interact (air, soil, water and sunlight) in a given area. In the Coastal Niger delta, the infections are due to the activities of oil companies causing the deterioration of the ecosystem (living environment) of the delta including the population human.

In fact, industrial activities and wastes they produce are discarded directly into the rivers, Swamps and Creeks or Ocean. We observed large surfaces of crude oil cakes covering the swamps, the plains, creeks and on the channels that made us to conclude and affirm it specially, around where oil fields and operational activities of the oil industry and other sub-sectors of the oil industry are sited. Some of these wastes are hazardous chemicals to the human health. These chemicals, including mercury compounds can cause serious and inexplicable illnesses and eventually cause death.

In 1988, in the Clan of Boma (Around Peremabiri, Diebu etc), a transmission oil pipe was broken which has poured millions of barrels of crude oil and toxic chemicals into the rivers, creeks and farm lands. Because many towns and villages in the delta do not even have drinking water (pipe borne water), the only domestic water is the water from the rivers or creeks or wells in the brackish water areas. The result of this oil spillage was hundreds of sick and claim many lives.

Another case was that of Egebiri in Tarakiri clan, again, there were severe cases and deaths. In all cases, the situation was always manages by paying ridiculous compensations to the affected towns which they called victims of the spillage. As in the case of Boma the some of 4,000,000 Naira [1] was paid. The compensation that was paid does not match the gravity of the damage cause to the ecosystem of the delta environment. No clean-up work was done either by the oil companies or any intervention from the Federal or State Governments for any clean-up works to be carried out. While preventive measures would have been better for the people and the ecosystem. These types of accidents are frequent that no one talks about it any more in the Delta today.

Pollution does not only affects humans and animals, but also plants and marine algae. Agricultural productivity has been severely affected causing environmental degradation vegeto-animal. Local fishing industries are no more operational due to poor productions (catches).

The pollution of the marine community[2] of the Niger delta is certainly one of the most dramatic alterations of environment, because ultimately the pollutants on land eventually reach the salt water through rivers and runoff from falling rain. But what are the factors of pollution in the waters of the Niger delta?

Schematically, the pollutants of environments in the Niger delta can be divided into three categories: (a) Domestic (b) Chemical-industrial and (c) Hydrocarbons.

The domestic contaminations are linked to major industrial cities like Port Harcourt, Warri, Sapele, Ughelli, Bonny, etc. These cities have large concentrations of populations therefore fundamentally pollution by organic matter associated with various pathogens including domestically use of detergents add to the actual chemical pollution.

The industrial chemical contaminations are more diverse. Direct discharges from chemical industries established on the coasts or on the fourteen major rivers of the delta are of much greater importance, such as acid or alkaline solutions from various manufacturing plants.

Finally, pollution from the hydrocarbons in the melancholy gained fame since 1957[3] following a series of rupture of a wellhead or oil pipes[4].

---

[1]   About 571,428.57 US dollars.

[2]   The brackish water area, the transition zone and its surroundings.

[3]   Year when oil was discovered for the first time in the delta.

[4]   Cf. supra above.

The increased oil drilling in the province results in damages to agricultural pollution and its affects people's health. The most disturbing result of the action in short or long term products discharged into natural environment of the Niger delta.

Chapter 5

The types of towns based on their morphological site

5.1.0. The major sites and growth centre

Aerial photos of the 1963 and 1964 at a scale: 1:100,000 enable us to classify the towns into two main groups according to their spatial morphology. These are towns that have a single centre homogeneous and those with multiple centres (fig 5.1). These centres are not necessarily represented the town centres, but centres of trade and economic activities. It appears in the light of observation that harmonious and comprehensive development based necessarily on a hierarchical network centre is likely to make their equipment to cope up with the entire population. In both categories (fig 5.1) for the entire delta, Sapele and Warri are the first category (*western delta*). These towns/cities are growing without any physical barrier to the changes of terrain or rivers, streams, but oblige a growth in length or extension. The second category, are towns that have developed from several villages in the proximity to each other or where the topographic factors obliged a development by spread.

Indeed, we observed two types of growth centre in this category (*the secondary category*): Those having multiple-centres (in one town) and those made-up of several towns or villages to form one town. The first are those represented by the sites of Amassoma, Buguma, Abonnema, Agbere, Peremabiri, Ahoada, etc (fig 5.2a). These are towns having multiple centres, but spread out from a single towns since the beginning of settlement. The second towns Port Harcourt (City), Okrika, Sabagria, Degema, Yenagoa, Opokuma, Odi, Kaiama, Nembe etc (fig 5.2b). These towns have grown from several town or villages that have come together during their development over time and have become one town today. Most of the settlements classified towns in the delta are in this category of towns today (for administrative purpose?) cf. figs 5.4, 5.5. Nevertheless, one can notice that the city of Port Harcourt has two centres[1]: Traditional on some areas and modern on the others (GRA). Each of these centres has their centres of economic activities. There exists very often a difference between the traditional and modern centres. Very often, where this difference is not remarkable, the centres traditional and modern are recognizable as the old centre and modern downtown (Ahoada). Their growth, planning and structure are the results of its economic, social and cultural standards, since the centres and the physical position are the qualities of the sites.

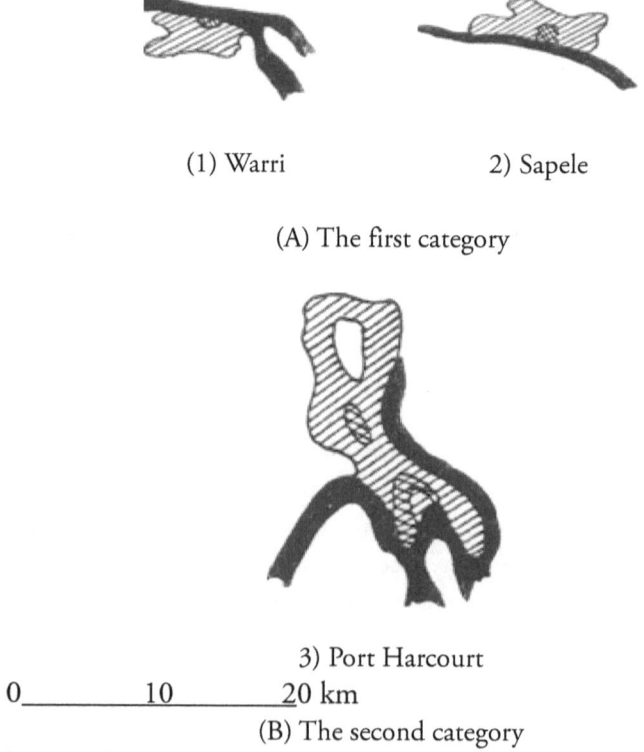

(1) Warri   2) Sapele

(A) The first category

3) Port Harcourt

0_____10_____20 km

(B) The second category

Fig 5.1: The category of growth centres in the Niger

---

[1]   Here the centre should be considered as areas (Government reserved Areas-GRA). These area are not concentrated in one area, but in different areas in the city.

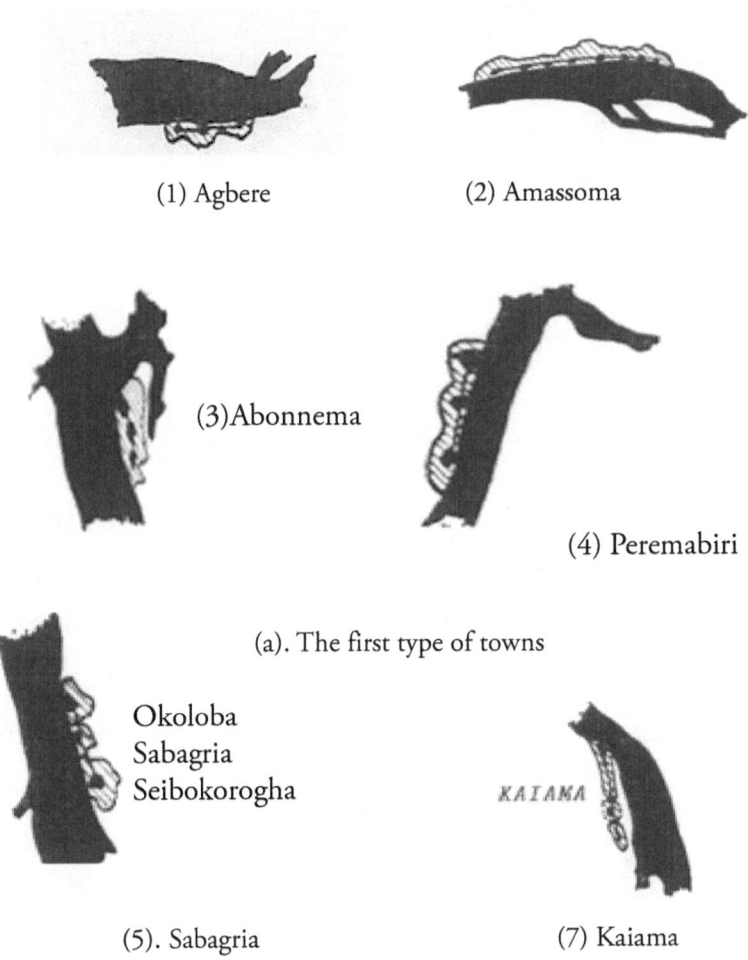

(1) Agbere   (2) Amassoma

(3)Abonnema

(4) Peremabiri

(a). The first type of towns

Okoloba
Sabagria
Seibokorogha

KAIAMA

(5). Sabagria   (7) Kaiama

0   30   60 km

Opu-Degema

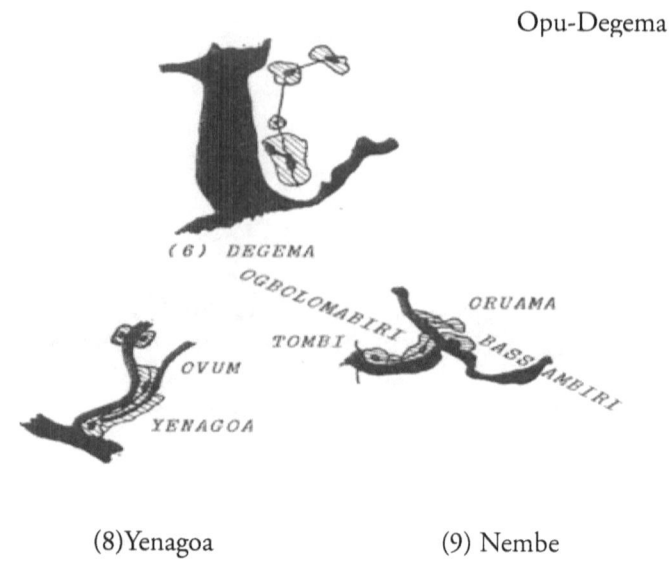

(8)Yenagoa   (9) Nembe

(b). The second type of towns

Fig 5.2: The types of growth centres in the second category of towns in the delta.

Considering each city in the delta as a whole in relation to the morphology of the sites, it consists of two main morphological forms. These represent the different types of sites in the Delta. In fact, the overall morphology of the delta evokes a sheet of brain anatomy with a multiple ramifications from the rivers drawing thousands of circumvolutions in the spongy tissue of the mangrove, the coastal mangroves and mashes of the interior of the delta. However, the locations (sites) of these two morphological types of towns vary according to where the observers are located: in the area of freshwater, Brackish water, or in the coastal zone.

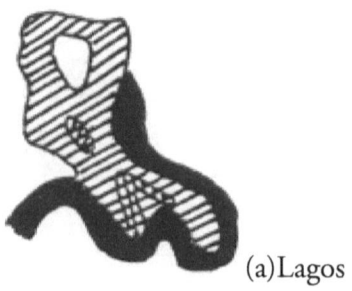

(a)Lagos

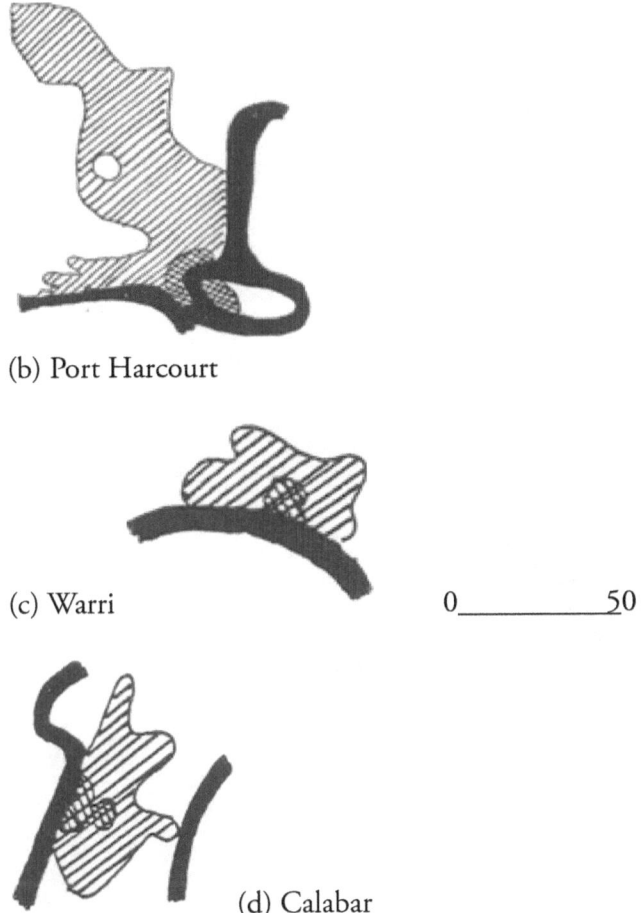

(b) Port Harcourt

(c) Warri   0_____50

(d) Calabar

Fig. 5.3: The major sites and the centres of growth of Nigerian coastal Cities.

Fig 5.3 shows that the morphologies of towns in the Niger delta are determined by topographical conditions. Looking closely to the spatial occupation of Lagos and Port Harcourt, show that both cities have a similar morphology.

Although, the freshwater zone of the Niger delta contains fewer creeks, swamps and rivers compared to the south of the delta (area of brackish water), but has much dry lands on the natural levee suitable for settlement. A visit on several towns in these areas reveals two types of spatial settlements (occupation): settlements in length (*along a river, lake etc*); settlements in depth (*from a river, a lake, stream etc*).

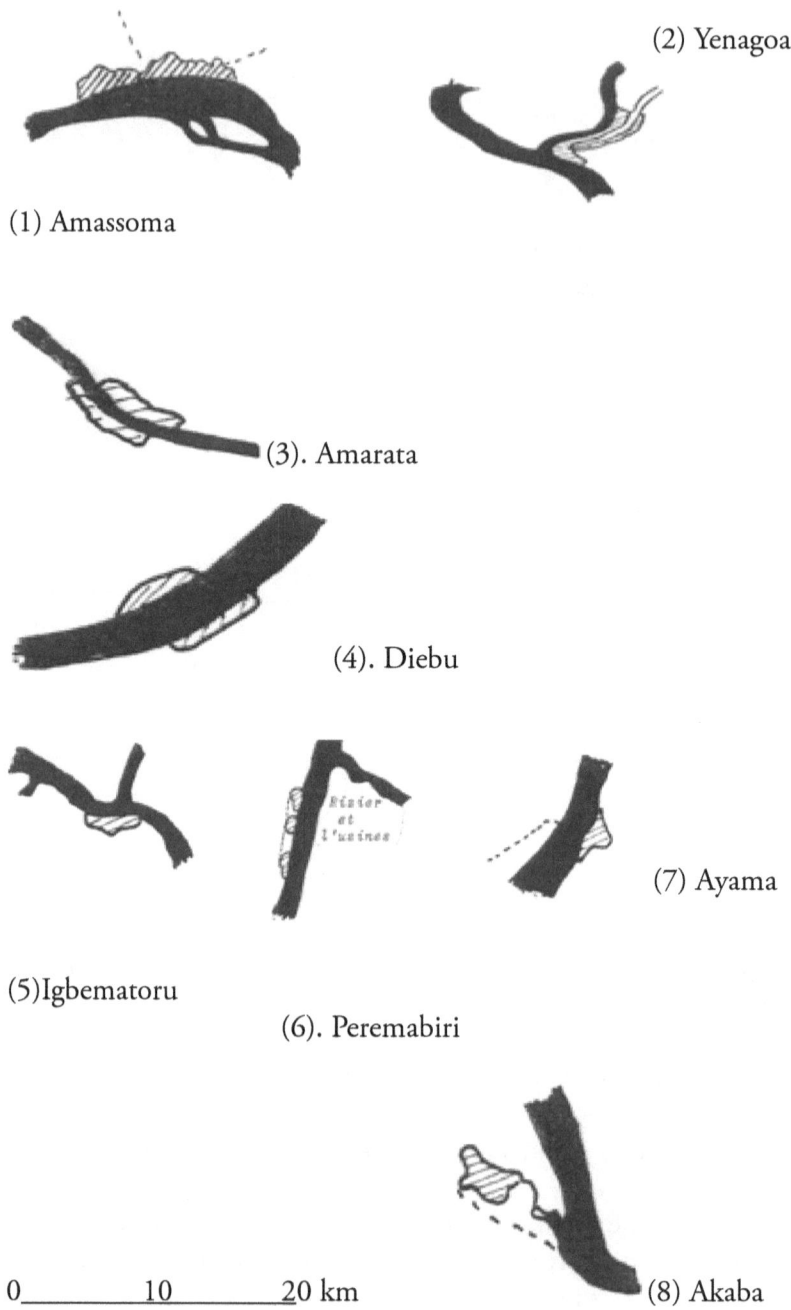

(2) Yenagoa

(1) Amassoma

(3). Amarata

(4). Diebu

(7) Ayama

(5)Igbematoru

(6). Peremabiri

0 _____ 10 _____ 20 km

(8) Akaba

Fig 5.4: The spatial morphology of the main towns in the freshwater area and transition zone.

Towns like Amassoma, Anyama and Kaiama whose settlements were in length are today developing in depth due to the construction of road to or passing it.

In general the sites of these towns are located on the concave parts of the rivers, in such away that one has a great view on both sides of the town as in the case of Amassoma, Odi, Sagbama, Kaiama, Oporoma, Buguma, Abonnema, Yenagoa, Sabagria, Patani, Kpakama, etc (fig 5.4 (1) (2) (6) (7) . . .). The sites of these towns are on naturally fairly elevated and of topographical and economic interest. The level of land slops as one moves away from the river, creek or stream, so that the rear of the town is a swamp or flood plain. An observation on the urban settlements revealed a characteristic length of these towns (At the natural levees (edge of rivers, creek etc) fairly high to escape the river flooding.

We can observe several canoes on the bank of the river. It is therefore possible that the second (Settlement in length) reasons for the settlement in length are related to have a space to anchor their canoes to their neighbourhoods.

The towns of in-depth settlement are characterized by having at least two means of transport, by road and river. That is these towns are either on the edge of a river, a creek and crossed by a road separating in two or more as in the case of Mbiama (fig 5.4(2)). We classify these towns as towns of the interior of the Niger delta. Like the towns on rivers Niger, Forcados, Nun etc of which the rears are still swamps. It is therefore obvious that to undertake any development and expansion of these towns needs some techniques for draining the marshes that are located around these towns.

5.2.0. The area of brackish water.

This zone occupies the south of the coastal Niger delta. The Niger River and Forcados River divide in to several branches: rivers Benin, Brass, Bonny, Cross, and other various rivers unit to form a labyrinth of creeks and lagoons. This part of the delta configuration has far more complex than the freshwater zone. It is covered with impenetrable (or very difficult) vegetation where cultivable land is scarce. The countless channels, inlets, estuaries and instability might have pushed the population to be segmented

---

[1]   Fresh or brackish water areas.

into multiple groups in search of good land for settlement. Most of the towns in this area have a settlement which is often in dept on a cordon of land (fairly high) with river or creek on both sides of the cordon of land (fig 5.5) Buguma and Abonnema. Good sites for settlement are generally located at the confluence of two rivers, a river and creek near the confluence like Degema, Buguma, Abonnema, Bakana, etc. Another morphological characteristic of towns in this area is that the sites are often on the convex side of the river or creeks (fig 5.5 (1.3), (1.2)).

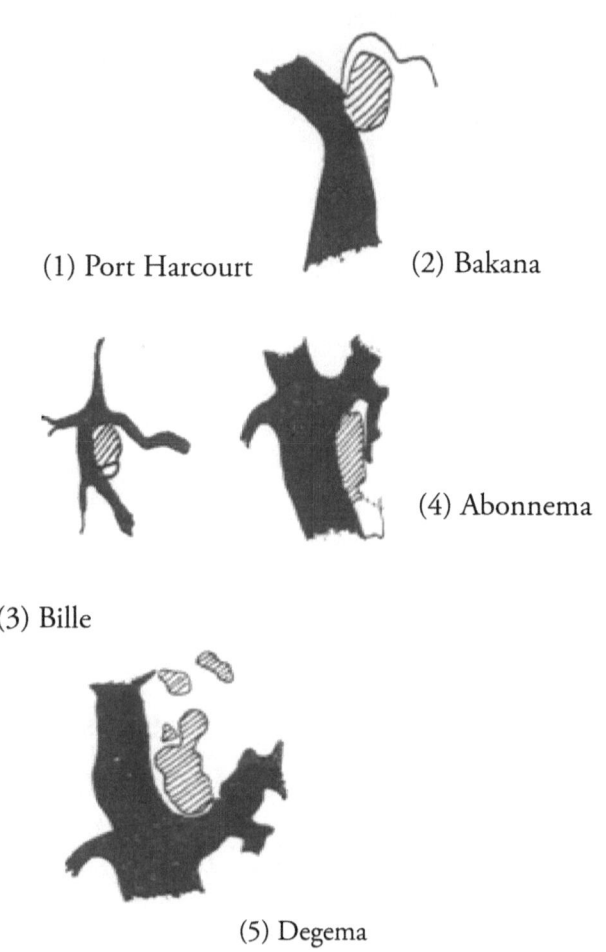

(1) Port Harcourt   (2) Bakana

(4) Abonnema

(3) Bille

(5) Degema

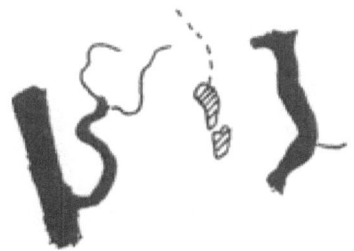

(6). Obonoma

Fig 5.5: The spatial morphologies of major towns in the brackish water area.

The last types of towns are those in retreat from the rivers or creeks or swamps. These cities are located on land high enough inside that the inhabitants prefer to build away from the edge of the river rather than lowlands example: Obonama, Elim, Eguama, Agudama-Epie (fig 5.5 (6)).

5.3.0. The coastal Zone

This area covers the entire coast of the Niger delta. Towns are masked by the barrier islands. The barrier islands are small islands at the mouth (estuaries) from the Ocean. In fact, towns have the same morphologies as the towns of the brackish water; the only difference is that, coastal towns are all in-depth with the old centre on the edge of the river or creek with the Atlantic Ocean behind the town (fig 5.5). Although, the mangrove limits and determines the morphology of the towns especially the marshes (wetlands), islands on which these towns are located are much larger and wider compared to other towns of brackish water.

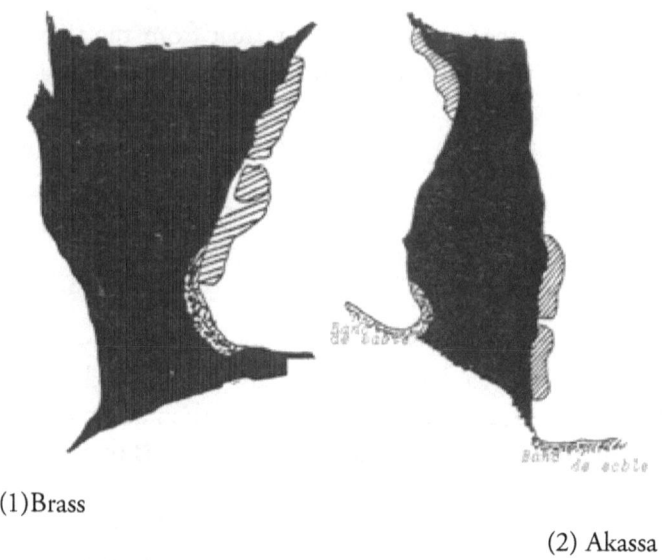

(1)Brass

(2) Akassa

Fig 5.6: The spatial morphologies of the main towns of the coastal zone of the Niger delta.

Chapter 6

The Administrative capacities of Community Development and planning in the Niger Delta.

6.1.0. A despised region?

The coastal Niger delta has for centuries been regarded as an amphibious area. However, no development project that takes into account the particularities of the region to improve their living environment was undertaken. Consequently, the peoples of the delta depend on themselves. Indeed, the authorities claimed that no development was possible and that the delta is under water (Eastern Region). Secondly, since early 1960s, Nigeria has been planning without facts and development planning was based on data values (tax records, population, economic etc).

However, the district administrative headquarters like Degema, Brass and Yenagoa had more advantages than the other towns, except those cities/towns developed during the colonial era such as Port Harcourt, Warri, Sapele, Bonny and Brass. These cities or towns are today become the major industrial and commercial or business cities.

In fact, in 1967[1] the administration of the eastern Delta came to the hands of the people of the Niger Delta[2] to be able to make their own

---

[1]   The year in which states were created in the Niger delta including "The Rivers State" in the eastern delta.

[2]   Who knows their problems of underdevelopment and planning they have been confronting since decades.

projects. They have now the hope to solve the environmental development and planning problems they have been confronting, since decades. The local authorities have greater advantages of having grants and direct funding from the Federal Government to enable local authorities to achieve their projects (community projects). Will the administrative and political policies of the State Government give the financial possibilities to enable these local Authorities to carryout their projects? Or will the Local Authorities use the funds as required of them? Finally, we hope and believe that the State and or Federal Governments are aware of today's challenges concerning the problems in the region and the possibilities to make global development taking in to account the particularities of the delta. Then what are the techniques for an effective global environmental development and planning in the delta?

6.2.0. Urbanization

Urbanization in Nigeria is not easy to describe with certainty in some degree, of one part by the lack of statistical data and material, the other by the character of cities. Most cities are not equipped with the services and the functions which are the minimum criteria for the classification as an urban area as in the developed countries, and their populations are often composed of farmers. Such areas can be found especially in the states[1] where there are scattered settlements of small populations with very little urban functions. It also applies to some areas in the Yoruba, Hausa and Igbo states. Except Lagos and Jos that had European influenced development and planning.

However, to understand urbanization in Nigeria in general, it is necessary to link urbanization to economic development. We can identify two phenomena that have maintained complex relationship with ambivalence that differentiate two categories of towns: the "*productive towns*" and "*non productive towns*".

Productive cities/towns are those that have positive influence for development of their region by their birth and growth (Port Harcourt in the Delta . . .). While the parasite cities/towns are the non productive

---

[1]   Composed of the States: Anambra, Akwa-Ibom, Bayelsa, Imo, Rivers, South of Delta (Delta State).

cities/towns and have no influence or beneficial development and growth of the region.

The towns of the eastern part of the country are of more recent origin and do not reflect traditional structures in the north with an exception of the Niger delta, despite the urbanization of their institutions. Consequently, it would be more accurate to consider the creation of cities as a phenomenon introduced by the colonization. They still remained relatively small, while spreading harmoniously in the landscape by maintaining a balance between the towns who could never qualify as a city.

At the eve of the creation of the Rivers State, Port Harcourt was the only planned city that had the qualification of 'the Garden City". A quality inherited from the colonizers (The British). But in the western delta, there were many, including Warri, Sapele etc. From this the infrastructures necessary for the implantation of industries were concentrated at the sole city of Port Harcourt (Eastern delta, Rivers State). This resulted in a polarization of economic activities in the State in the sole dominant centre.

Under this limitative situation, the Authorities pursued a particular policy of urbanization and development to create new centres as growth poles in other parts of the State other than Port Harcourt. This politic was pursued by the various successive administrations, often with very significant changes from the predecessors. The first part of the politic of urbanization is the modification of the law N° 1è of 1960 which allowed the creation of 17 local Government areas from the existing five districts (fig 5.1).

Indeed, the Local Government administration in the eastern part of the delta is an adaptation and modification of the system of the former eastern region before the creation of River State in May 27, 1967. However, the administrative centres of the new districts were designated as urban centres (see Appendix V & fig 8.1). For the continuation of this politic of urbanization, a study commission was formed in 1972 to prepare a master plan for these newly created Local Governments area headquarters: Ahoada, Bori, Brass and Degema. In the following year (1973), 10 others were created their master plans were also prepared they are: Abua, Bonny, Isiokpo, Nchia, Ogbia, Okechi, Okrika, Ukubie, Omoku, Oporoma Rumuogha, Taabaa, Yenagoa and in parallel another master plan for the State Headquarter, Port Harcourt (covering a radius of 24 km).

The year 1974 saw an expansion of urban planning. However, 19 packages or detailed plans were made for the towns of Abonnema, Akassa,

Bodo, Buguma, Igbomatoru, Ighuraka/Agwa/Ipo, Kolo, Tombia and Umuotoru. At the end of the second National development plan, the state Government has standardized 35 detailed urban plans sets with a budget of 3 millions of Naira. For the realization of these projects, 18 planning authorities were form by the State Government. 703 plots were allocated in all residential areas and 142 commercial plots were allocated to industrialists at the end of budget year of 1975-76. Most of the plots allocated to the industrialists are now built up.

Another important part of urban planning was the shooting of aerial photographs to draw the maps of the local Governments areas. This was completed at the end of 1976. A workshop was set up within the Ministry of Lands and Housing for the mapping of these areas.

Although, these efforts have been made by the administration of the first Military Governor of the State (His Excellency Commander Alfred Diete-Spiff), the State was still underdeveloped compared to other States in the country. This was probably due to the frequent changes of its Governors after first Military Governor that had no enough time and these projects are never followed up by their predecessors, so lacks continuity of the project assets on his arrival to the office. This makes us beginners of projects, but hardly terminates them.

However, the urbanization of towns in the Niger delta continues with the policy of rural industrialization and the new administrative structure of the delta (fig 6.1) (they are now more than 14). That? We force ourselves to believe.

In addition, the utilities board is responsible for the extension and installation of public equipment particularly electric power, supply of drinking water etc However, a massive rural electrification program using natural gas turbines for the electrification of fifty towns and villages in two Local Government areas: Yenagoa (YELGA) and Ahoada (ALGA) fig 8.1. A second gas turbine was to be installed at Buguma, set for the electrification of all such important towns in the Degema Local Government area.

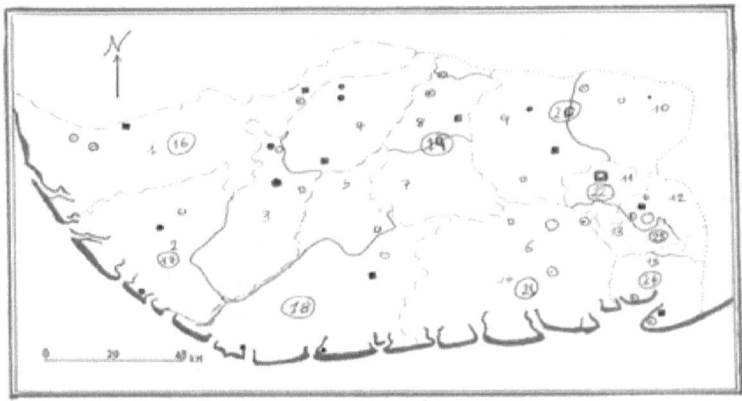

▣ Capital of Rivers State (Port Harcourt)
▪ Local Government Area (Headquarters)
⬤ Major towns
⊙ Flood & Erosion control projects (Completed)
○ Land reclammation projects (Completed)
•   Dam
–·– LGA Boundaries in 1973
⤳ LGA Boundaries in 1989

Urban Councils 1973: (1) Sagbama (Bendel State before 1973), (2) Kuluama-Ukubie, (3) Oporoma-Oporoma, (4) Yenagoa-Yenagoa, (5) Ogbia-Ogbia, (6) Brass-Brass, (7) Abua/Odual-Abua, (8), Ahoada-Ahoada, (9) Ikwerri-Isiokpo, (10) Etche-Okehi, (11) Obio-Rumuogbo, (12) Tai/Eleme-Nchia, (13) Okrika-Okrika, (14) Kalabari-Degema, (15) Bonny-Bonny.

LGAs 1989: (16) Sagbama-Sagbama, (17) Yenagoa-Yenagoa, (18) Brass-Brass, (19) Ahoada-Ahoada (20) Elele-Isiokpo, (21) Degema-Degema, (22) Port Harcourt-Port Harcourt, (23) OTELGA-Nchia (24) OLGA-Bonny.

Fig 6.1: The Local Government Areas, their capitals (1973 and 1989) and development projects (soil reclammation, erosion and flood control) in the study area.

6.3.0. Community development

It is impossible today to discuss on community development in the Coastal Niger Delta without emphasizing Government action. There may be an opportunity for the people of the province or almost completely unknown in the world to be able to develop their towns in the future.

Indeed, development projects financed by the local authorities before are today financed by the State Government. However, the Government intervenes in three cases:

1. The first case the Government participate on the establishment and technical assistance of the project which belongs fully or partially to the Government (financing).
2. The second case is to distribute grants, technical assistance or advice, tools etc. such as subsidies for farmers, hospitals, health centres, dispensaries, Schools, markets or even self-help cooperative societies and investment projects.
3. The State Government is the sole owner of the project and awards contracts for its realization.

The policy pursued in terms of planning community sites by the Government consisted in recent years to focus on the draining of swamps, creating channels to create shortcuts on waterway transport routes[1] and road infrastructures etc, but some of these projects were highly beneficial to the south of the delta. Outside of these projects by the Government of the state, and the local Authorities, there were other planning authorities created by the Federal Government with the participation of all the development Authorities in the State. These are: The Niger Delta Development Board (N.D.D.B) and the Niger Delta Basin Development Authority (N.D.B.D.A) (Appendices III).

There are four main problems facing this region concerning development and planning. They are: flooding, erosion, swamps and transport. The objective of the N.D.D.B reflects these four issues. These development boards were replaced by another, created in 1976 to continue

---

[1]   Only the southern part of the delta benefited from these projects. Mainly the area of brackish water.

with the same mission and objectives with slight additions (agriculture as its priority).

To this end, it needs to control floods, erosion and the means of transport for the agricultural products which reflects our research area. Among the projects launched by the body[1], ten were completed. Although its mission is the development of agriculture in the region to provoke rural development by collective planning and management of projects that reflect the geographic and economic realities of the region.

6.3.1. Completed projects(see appendix III)

(a) The project of growing rice at Peremabiri: This project cover an area of 1,300 hectares of land for the cultivation, but needed irrigation in other to cultivate in all seasons.

(b) Development of fish farming: this project covers an area of 4,000 hectares located in several communities in the delta including Bodo, Buguma (Federal Fisheries), Ekowe, and Polobugo.

(c) The Sagbama river project (on river Forcados).

(d) Isampou rice project.

(e) Control against flooding and erosion.

(f) Rural water supply.

(g) Yenagoa palm oil plantation.

(h) Andoni river project.

(i) Development of modern and artisan fishing.

(j) Nun River projects (the raphia palm project).

(k) Construction of wharves, land reclamation and development of rivers for navigation.

(l) The development of local Government area headquarters.

(m) The development of poultry.

To carry out these and other projects, an Institute for flood, erosion, soil reclamation and technology attached to Rivers State University of Science and Technology and the Ministry of agriculture make the theoretical and practical research. This simplifies the task for the organizations and the Authorities dealing with public utilities in the State.

---

[1]   The N. D. B. D. A—Niger Delta Basin Development Authority.

The popular practice of collective planning and management of a site is in someway the most economical and interesting (minor projects). It involves the active participation of the inhabitants and organised by the people themselves. The work lasts from one to three days or more (man and women are all involve). One of these projects was carried out at Amassoma (East) which consisted in the refilling a channel dug for shrimp fishing. Aimed in away to fight against flooding the rear of the town. This channel has been for many years one of the causes of the flooding in the town.

The materials used were buckets, shovels, hoes and clay as backfill with which the channel was covered up for a length of about 200 metres in May 1976. However, its years of activity have brought more sediment to the area, but more disaster than good. That is the elevating the swamp level over about 30 acres of wetlands despite the damages it caused during its activity and the disadvantages. Many other projects were carried out in other towns in this manner against erosion, flood problems or drying small areas.

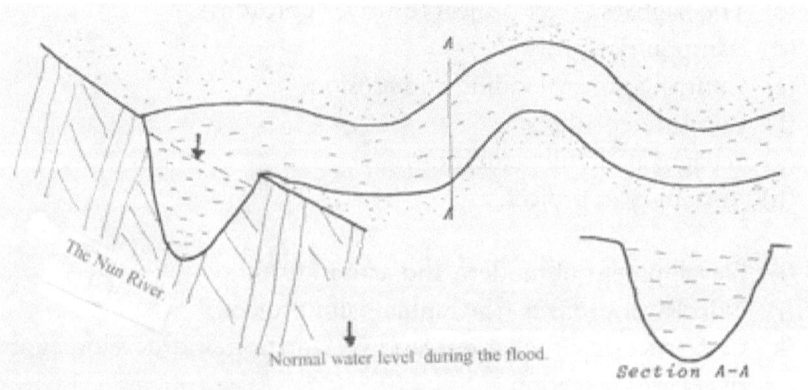

Normal water level during the flood.

Section A-A

Fig 6.2: The channel (Eretu-oba) for shrimp fishing.

6.4.0. The Administrative capacity and planning policies

The administrative and collective planning policies of the region has come to the hands of the peoples of the Niger delta. These are: Rivers State, Bayelsa State (on the East); Delta State (on the west) and the Niger Delta Development Authority (Federal Government). In addition to these are individual efforts. In the western Delta which is part of Delta state (formerly Bendel) levels, we have nine local government Areas. They are Bomadi, Burutu, Ethiope, Isoko, Ndokwa, Okpa, Ughelli, Warri and Sapele (fig 8.3). There are thirty Local Government Areas in the Eastern Niger Delta: 22 in Rivers State and 8 in Bayelsa State. See appendices II.

The Authorities of the State maintain a permanent contact with the local Government Authorities for the administration and planning policies through the Community Development Committees. These Committees have many functions. Among these functions are: Direction of food, road and rural infrastructures, planning and urban development, protection of public utilities in the towns. Its mission is to advise the Municipalities' development projects and recommends projects for the local Government to the State Government for its approval and implementation.

As for the Niger Delta Basin Development Authority which was one of the 11 Authorities for the development of rivers in Nigeria, established by Decree 37 of August, 1976. Its mission is to increase the living conditions of the rural populations and the need for attention to problems of rural development. They replaced the Niger Delta Development Board, created in the 60s whose mission was to study the possibilities of developing the Coastal Niger Delta, particularly its stationary economy.

The functions of the N. D. B. D.A (appendices III), among others is to undertake a detailed development of all ground water for multiple uses, to undertake projects for the fight against floods etc. It is also to assist the local Government Authorities for the implementation of rural development projects in its areas of operation or under its authority. The N. D. B. D. A. covers the entire State of Rivers (now Rivers and Bayelsa) and the southern part of Delta State (formerly in Bendel State)[1]. Project funding in the case C. D. C is by the State Government and in the case of N.D.B.D.A is by the Federal Government. However, N. D. B. D. A. receives grants from the Federal budget.

6.5.0. The popular Local Methods of project funding.

There are various forms depending on the method employed, specific to each town or village. But, in general, the authorities of the town

---

[1]   The Niger Delta is the largest delta in Africa and has an area of 39,269 km^2 of which 19049 km^2 are under the authority of N. D. B. D. A.

organized a launching ceremony, inviting VIPs, businessmen/women etc. During these ceremonies that the public, the invitees are requested to donate towards the project, they have announced earlier. The funds thus obtained are then used either to begin the project or if it has already started, then is to complete the project.

Other methods are more traditional in the way of individual contributions. A fixed sum is set (for males and for females) respectively of the town, even if that person lives at Lagos as far as he or she is in the country (Nigeria). This type of financing by personal contribution is mandatory for all the citizens of the town.

Such projects belong to the town, but if the town can no longer be able to implement the project due to financial insufficiency, then the CDC intervene, so that the local Government takes charge of the project in question.

Chapter 7

The Government Strategies in urban Planning in the Niger Delta

The natural element and phenomena, which are imposed in the delta makes that the inhabitants do not cease looking for ways to have a better living environment and to fight for solutions to them: floods, erosion.

To get the facts to respond to the various development and planning sectors, the inhabitants organized themselves for massive participation (self help projects) in development programs. However, in each community is always formed a planning committee whose members are from the community. The community gives the initiative of the projects and mobilizes residents for their execution. All these efforts are to make life easier for themselves, particularly in the fields of communication, planning, and land use, health, social work, and education etc.

7.1.0. The strategies of the Administrations of the delta

The landscape features of the Niger delta makes that the inhabitants are obliged to undertake planning strategies appropriate to their locality (region). The dramatically symbolic cardinal characteristic push to rural development is the creation of the Directorate of food and rural infrastructure (DFRRI) (fig 7.1). Its mission is to accelerate the development of rural areas in the construction of all the leads connected to sewers, water supply, in the development of agriculture in the construction of other infrastructures. Another feature is the recognition of community development committee (CDC) as an important Agent of development.

Anyway, the DFRRI depends on the CDC for its effectiveness and firmness. CDC is in permanent contact with the people to give them the necessary motivations for progress of their town. It also motivates the people to make donation of land and land preparation for the projects. These accelerate the rapid take off of projects. Other rural development Agencies[1] other than the DFRRI are the State Government, local Authorities, and authorities of the Niger Delta Basin Development, private companies on contract bases with the Government.

In fact, the DFRRI works in parallel with those of the local authorities to render additional services.

D. F. R. R. I

D F R R I

capital)

(Federal

(Federal capital)

D. F. R. R. I

D F R R I

capital)

(State

(State capital)

D. F. R. R. I

(Local Authorities capital)

C. D. Cs   C. D. Cs

(a) Linking D. F. R. R. I to C. D. Cs   (b) Linking

DFRRI to the capital of local Authorities

Table 7.1: The flow chart of D.F.R.R.I and its link to C. D. Cs

The Federal Government's interest in rural development, see the creation of the rural accelerated integrated rural development programme

---

[1]   At national level, the coastal Niger Delta is still considered a rural area, so only the rural developments programs that are assigned to this region (the Coastal Niger Delta).

(RAIRDEP)[1]. Since the second republic, the country's economic situation, not one agency Government agent, to undertake development projects and planning for the improvement of the living conditions in the region. However, the mission of RAIDEP is to group the resources of several agents of developments and planning in order to complete the implementation of a particular purpose. For example in the auspices of RAIRDEP drilling equipment[2] for water supply in the communities, the bulldozers were purchased, a major investment for the development of agricultural programs. As a result, the RAIRDEP exists in all development agents including the people who pay the taxes (development fees) to CDCs together.

The RAIRDEP aimed largely to problems in different areas of local authorities, especially fresh water, cleaning of agricultural land, industrial-property in each local authority area (fig 7.2).

Military Governor						
			RAIRDEP			
	Government			Public Sector		
mwt	mlg	Federal Agents	dfrri	cdc Villages	coy* State Level	po *club, Unions, Association

Source: CDC guide, Rivers State Ministry of Information, Port Harcourt.

*M.W.T=Ministry of Works and Transport; M.L.G= Ministry of Local Government; C.O.Ys = Companies; P.Os=Public Organizations.

Table 7.2: The Flowchart RAIRDEP

The importance of the Niger delta for economy of the country is the presence of crude oil due the geographical and geological structures. Unfortunately, the richness of the oil is not used for the development of the province. Even the oil companies have little or no concern about the daily damages coursed to the eco-system of the Delta environment.

---

[1]   Created during the administration of Col. A.S.I Ukpo, the Military Governor of Rivers State in General Babangida's era as well as DFRRI and the CDCs.

[2]   For the boreholes for drinking water.

However, the Niger delta is still considered a rural area, although there are towns that are in size and population could be classifies as urban areas.

In fact, the strategy of rural development is to improve the economy and social life of the rural population, that is to say reducing rural poverty. This involves the extension of public services and the benefits of development to rural areas[1]. It is with this objective that the inhabitants of the Niger delta have been fighting for the improvement, production, growth and productivity. The most important of all is to benefit fully from the oil produce in their land.

However, the inhabitants are aware that amelioration of all food products, nutrition and basic services such as health, education and communications do not provide alone, the best management and quality of life (poverty) rural, can contribute to improving productivity and their share in the economy of the province.

In this context, the objective of the inhabitants is for the development of their region to cover more than just a particular sector. They want the Government to improving productivity, creating employment and thus income growth per capita to a minimum acceptable with regard to food, communication, health education and housing. And the oil companies to participate actively in local development programs, construction of roads, schools, health centres, dispensaries etc. These are not expensive for an oil company to embank on. They are exploiting the underground wealth of the area, and suppose to make at least a little effort to please the people who are suffering from their activities.

The original configuration of the Niger delta, its topography, morphology and its special amphibious (two-thirds) characteristic, the immediate vicinity of the ocean, the presence of excess rivers constituting as many problems[3] as making communication especially challenging and difficult.

However, one of the main objectives of the authorities is to provide as many channels of communication and transport (navigation)[4] to facilitate the transportation problems in the region. Thus, the Rivers State mass transit service was inaugurated in October 1988. The service's mission is to buy more vessels to the existing ones in the inland waterways. In the

---

[1]   Among others to benefit from these areas are farmers, those without cultivable land and the unemployed.

[2]   One town to another.

[3]   One town to another.

[4]   Road and water transport.

road transport, new buses were purchased[1] in addition to existing ones by the Ministry of Transports. Further more, the determination of the people to open rural areas to develop agriculture and industry, are committed to the construction of new roads vital (fig 7.3) which are either under construction, completed or planned including roads:

(1) Edepie—Imiringi—Emeyal.
(2) East-West—Sagbama
(3) Igbegene—Polaku
(4) Nchia—Ogigbo
(5) Abonnema—Obonoma
(6) Omoku—Omudioga—Okehi—Eberi
(7) Ndoki—Umuagkai

In addition, the delta is linked to other States by air, road, and ocean. Port Harcourt has an international airport with regular flights to Lagos, Calabar, Enugu, Kaduna, Benin etc. There are also operating weekly flights to London, Rome and other major cities of Europe and other countries around the world via Lagos. But there are very few overseas direct flights from Port Harcourt. Communication with other States in the country is by road, railways and also by boat within the delta.

Fig 7.1: Road communication network

---

[1]   15 in 1988.

7.2.0. The health status of the towns in the Niger Delta.

After the creation of Rivers State in the Niger Delta, it was normal that the fight against transmissible diseases in the towns was at the forefront of the authorities.

The diseases like measles, malaria, dysentery, plague, whooping cough, pneumonia, cholera and venereal diseases were still a heavy toll. One[1] for instance estimated 24,410 the number of people infected with malaria in 1984 only 20 people with cholera. This represents only the cases registered in the public health institutions, but in reality is by far more than this figure.

The current major health problems of the towns in the Niger delta can only be assessed as a study or field observation and it is mainly at the beginning of the rainy season and floods. The official statistical data about this on the delta towns published by the Federal Ministry of health Lagos is not complete. Indeed, in all towns of the delta, diarrhoeal diseases occupy the first position, followed by malaria. It turns out that the diarrhoea, protein-energy malnutrition and other deficiency diseases, especially those of children are closely associated with poverty, ignorance, overcrowding and poor hygiene. They are constantly aggravated by rapid population growth, for example at Yenagoa, some residential areas of Port Harcourt etc.

Yenagoa is a town whose population does not cease to grow over the past decades due to its geographic situation and as a capital of a state (Bayelsa). Unfortunately, Yenagoa has a health situation precarious. In fact, there is no pipe borne water supply throughout the town, except some parts of the town (less than 35%). The population for this reason, there are those that depend on their personal boreholes and sell water, those that near the creek get theirs from the creek for domestic use while buy for drinking and cooking. The population is so used to the system, that people careless. I could see a principle of "what cannot be avoided can be endured". They can not avoid drinking or need water, so they endure its lacking and gets it by other means. This exposes the people to diseases like cholera, for example. Most of the streets and passages that serve as streets/closes are places where they throw garbage etc. And since

---

[1]   Federal Ministry of health, Port Harcourt, Annual Abstracts of Statistics, Lagos 1987.

most of the houses (traditional) are built[1] at ground level, there is always moisture throughout the year in major parts of the town. The houses are built without any town planning regulations, very dense and most of them without toilets. Part of the population uses the creek, forest (fallow land) and dumps as latrines. Faeces are also thrown directly into the creek/river[2] and since the water in the creek (almost stationary) or river it represents the risks for the population that uses this water from the creek or river for domestic purposes. As a result, the health of the population is under the constant risk conditions of transmissible diseases due to lack of equipment and hygiene environment.

Health services are spread over all Local Government Authority areas to meet the demands of health attention of the populations. These include hospitals, health centres, cottage hospitals of general medical practice[3], teaching hospitals, dispensaries and clinics (fig 7.2). At Port Harcourt, which is the third largest industrial city of the Federation, after Lagos and Kaduna, there are two large hospitals, Braidwaite memorial Hospital and Niger Hospital.

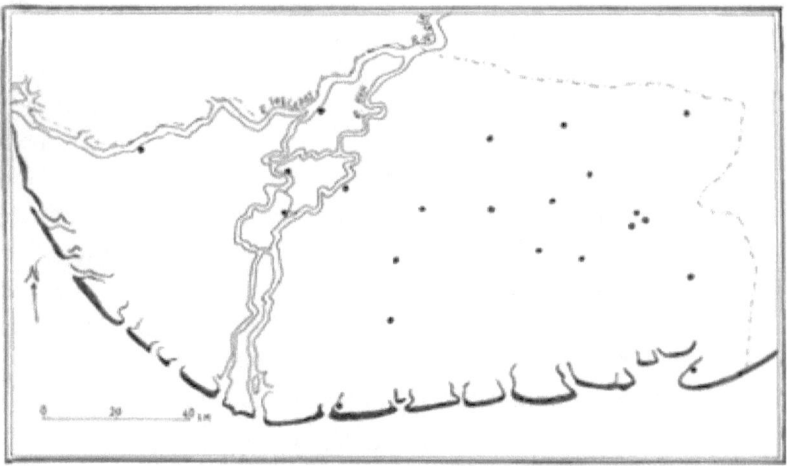

Fig 7.2: The distribution of hospitals/health centres (1989) in the area studied.

[1] This system is improving. Is a question of time the damp proof course (DPC) will be raised above the natural surface of the soil level (outside)

[2] It is practice largely all over most of the towns in the delta.

[3] Hospital where serious cases are not treated.

To these are added university hospitals, Federal medical centres and private Clinics, including the sea side Clinic, Poly Clinic, Teme Clinic, Santana Clinic, just to mention but few. There were 12 hospitals in the territory of the Niger delta (East) before the creation of Rivers State. Twenty-one hospitals were constructed in1976 (fig 7.2), There was also the construction of a school for Nurses and midwives at Rumueme near Port Harcourt (1976). Students of the school which are 60 to 100 are to be distributed to health institutions at the end of their studies. Other health institutions are Rumuigbo psychiatric hospital, school of hygiene and 250-bed maternity[1] and a hospital for children.

Finally, there is a particular service in this province, the 'flying Doctor service' created in 1975. These services are mandated to serve the towns or villages and serve Nembe, Terek, Kperikiri, Oloibiri, Egbematoru, Ekowe, Peremabiri, Akassa served by the hospital boat: Kala-Ekule while the Florence Nightingale is active in the Districts of Koluama. But we do not know, if these services still exist today. However, there is a discrepancy between health care institutions and the needs identified in certain areas of the province. Thus the problems associated with travel for kilometres for patients to be hospitalised are only partially resolved.

In Education, there are four Universities (study Area). The University of Science and Technology was founded in 1971 and obtained University status in 1980 with 310 lecturers and 3400 students. A second university was opened by the Federal Government, the University of Port Harcourt in 1975 with 337 lecturers and 3776 students. Other academic Institutions are colleges of Education that awards degrees and certificates and a School of Health Technology, School of Nursing, several technical colleges and high schools and a preparatory school for university entrance. Another University was established in 2000 (the Niger Delta University) by the Bayelsa State Government funded university located at Amassoma at about 30 kilometres from Yenagoa (the State capital); with an initial intake of 1039 students to a thriving population of more than 10,000 students and 3518 academic and non-academic staff with a College of Health Sciences.

There was a mass creation of Secondary schools in several towns at the same period. All were called Government Secondary Schools. And finally primary schools were opened in almost all towns and villages. The State

---

[1] All hospitals have maternity or at least one service even maternity clinics and polyclinics.

Government was to eradicate illiteracy or at least to the minimum in the State. An additional educational programs were made for adults (Adult education), but this was not successful. Upon all these efforts, there was still inadequacy in needs for teachers.

The electricity and water supplies are one of the priorities of the people/Government for centuries. There was no electricity and water supply in the towns. I mean regular energy supply. However, they used water from the rivers for domestic uses for towns in the freshwater areas while towns situated in the brackish water area rely on well water. There are very few that are linked to the national grid such as Warri, Sapele, Ughelli etc. At Port Harcourt light supply is also never regular.

As a result, the Government of the Rivers State launched a rural electrification project during Chief Milford OKILO's regime. This project is intended to provide an output of 40 megawatts of electricity and is supplied by gas turbines. 40 towns have already electricity, but the strategies will continue until all towns are supplied, if the project is not interrupted as in some cases for any change of administration.

7.3.0. Town and regional planning (photo7.1).

At the time of creation of Rivers State, Port Harcourt was the only city that has had the status of a planned urban centre. However, there were a number of cities that were by their functions could have been classified as urban centres, but in reality they are not. As a result, the infrastructures necessary for the implantation of industries are concentrated in the only city of Port Harcourt. This means a polarization of the economic activities in a single dominant centre.

In order to solve this problem, the Government has pursued a policy of urbanization and development to create new centres and the creation of growth centres in some of the other towns. This policy continues until today, which gives a satisfactory result.

Photo 7.1: The Port Harcourt—Aba Highway (Azikiwe Road)

7.4.0. Land reclamation (Photo 7.1)

We have mentioned in our first three chapters, the constraints of the Niger Delta.

(a)   (b)

(a). New land created by the drying up in Port Harcourt (Nembe waterside). One can notice the old waterside of sloping bank to the left of the photo and herbs that have begun to grow on the new earth created.

(b). New land created by drying up at Borikiri, Port Harcourt

Photo 7.2: The draining of marshes (land reclamation) in Port Harcourt for the construction of housing

7.5.0. Protection against flooding and erosion

During our fieldwork, we found that flooding and erosion are more constraining and degrading to the landscape in the freshwater than the brackish water area. Except in the coastal area where the erosion is much faster because of the waves of the Atlantic Ocean.

Really, two projects were launched, one on planning against erosion and the other against flooding. These two projects have not been giving an encouraging result, because the projects would have been appropriate for fresh water area. The brackish water areas are affected by high and low tides. Therefore a project adapted to the area would have worked out. However, the strategy of these developments continues by the competent Authorities in the matter, but can still be hampered by financial problems or a time slips.

A Delta is simply a river month in a sea or a lake. The Niger Delta is a delta, but composed of more than twelve rivers overlooking the Atlantic Ocean. In fact, the Niger Delta consists of a multitude of islands, rivers, creeks swamps are the cement of the mesh. However, the first urban solution is quite natural and is a choice between suitable settlement sites. That is why the settlements are often situated along highest plains (levees) or land plains of rivers, creeks, or lakes. The morphology of the plains is a land element in determining the types and morphology of the town. The Niger delta, however, split into two areas: the area of freshwater in the north and the area of brackish water in the south and the zone we have defined as the "*transition zone*", a zone between the two areas. Thus, the morphology of the towns is based on what area they are in freshwater or brackish water area.

Despite all the problems such as natural, topographical, the inhabitants have always sought for solutions to improve their living conditions. They have made great efforts to curb the natural effects or at least an improvement. The strategy of the delta people is to make life easier in transport and communication, urban/regional planning and development, health and social action. Like any other developing country governments, there are financial deviations in some projects planned for towns in the delta. The result is usually uncompleted projects, constructions etc while the contractor has unfortunately been paid completely. This is a financial moorage incurable transmissible disease in our society that disables effective development and planning.

The administrative strategies and Government policies are orientated towards development, infrastructure improvement, water supply, constructions of roads, lead connected, agriculture to facilitate rural-urban relationship. But are the inhabitants (contractors) ready to assimilate the rapid progress of DFRRI (Government efforts) initiatives in other to achieve rapid development in the region? This question remains unanswered as in some towns over 90% of the projects launched were not completed successfully. The Government will pay quite alright the totality of the contract, and the next Government will award another contract for the same project, so the same project keeps repeating for years. A good example is our case study.

Urban dynamics of the coastal Niger Delta

The coastal Niger delta was traversed by two English brothers, Richard and John Landers that were sent by the British Government in 1830. There were already upon their arrival, small towns and kingdoms in the delta. What is their origin? How were these towns created? Were they not developed from villages to towns? The existence of the towns could be linked to their profession and activities, particularly fishing and trade or linked to other factors such as refuge. All are conditioned by the nature of the morphology of the locations. For example Warri was said to be founded by the son of the Oba of Benin (refuge). He found it, because there were already inhabitants, the peoples who created the town before his arrival with his solders. And Port Harcourt, the capital of Rivers State was on commercial purpose by Harcourt in 1912.

The urban dynamic in the delta towns is characterise through a process of progressive settlements, from villages to towns, population growth, economic activities and the nature of relationships in networks.

The Niger delta is an area covered with impenetrable amphibious vegetation where cultivable dry land is rare[1]. The vegetation density, multitude of channels, creeks, estuaries and rivers has led to the settlement in multiple groups (villages). Indeed, the towns of the delta can be considered as a point in a vast space where reigns water, creeks, channels, swamps and floodplains.

The settlement in the Niger delta itself or the formation of the small city states and kingdoms has probably started after the establishment of the Benin Empire. Therefore, it becomes interesting to study the causes and significance of this concentration in the delta where agricultural activities are almost impossible. Where do they come from? Why in the delta? This leads us to the study of the peoples of the delta and their political organizations in chapter eight.

---

[1]   In view of their staple food crop in the region, which is contrary in Asia (The Tokin) delta where the staple food is rice. However, the alluvial deposits are widely used. Anyway, the Governments in the Niger delta in recent years have encouraged the cultivation of rice.

The inhabitants of the delta are from origin, fishermen, and producers of alcohol, salt, which they obtained from the salt water and canoe carvers. With arrival of the Europeans, they took the position of intermediaries in the slave trade between the Europeans and the traders from other parts of the country.

Since the intervention of the treaty of the slave trade and the colonization of the delta, urban growth was progressive throughout the region. The introduction of the legitimate trade led to a Significant decline in the urban growth in some towns in the Niger delta, including the towns in the estuaries (mouth of rivers) such as Bonny, until 1963, urban centres numbered four, in 1989, they exceeded 35, and the urban population increased from about 224,000 inhabitants (13.83%) in 1960, to about 922,000 inhabitants (23.76%) in 1989. This brings us to the study of the population growth in chapter nine.

Today, the activities of the delta inhabitants are growing and are diversified, for example, public transport (River, road etc), and types of business. This leads us to the study of the economic and commercial activities of the delta people and their standards of living in chapter ten.

Housing (accommodation) problems has increased in the recent years, mostly in the State capitals Port Harcourt (Rivers State), Yenagoa (Bayelsa State). Similarly, in the new administrative headquarters of the Local Government Areas lack accommodation.

However, these accommodation problems are less critical outside the cities and administrative headquarters, exception of some towns with high population. By cons, housing depends on the taste and choice, quality and type of accommodation that the future tenant would like to rent. In any case, it is easier to find an accommodation than at Port Harcourt, its agglomerations and Yenagoa. We will analyse it in chapter eleven.

Last and not the least, the system of relations in the delta are characterized by local markets, political, and administrative means. However, in some towns the market is daily while others, is weekly. Frequenting these markets round create relationships between them especially women who frequents the markets more than men. These relationships in addition to those from influential towns and attraction due to political and administrative or economic form a network of relationships. These will bring us to the analysis of the systems of urban relation network in chapter twelve.

Chapter 8

The people of the Niger delta and their political organization

8.1.0. The people of the Niger Delta

Nigeria is composed of a multitude of tribes and each of them can be defined as one group, of the same language, almost of the same custom and religion in general, the same civilization and very often of the same ancestors. For example of tribes: Efik, Igbo, Ijaw, Hausa and Yourba, in the North and West respectively.

The Niger delta is occupied by the tribes (ethnics) Ijaw (Izon), the Itsekiri, Urhobo and the Isokos. The last three are all in the west of the delta (fig 8.2 and 8.3). The Ijaw, the ethnic group dominant occupies the south of the Delta State and almost all of Rivers State with five other minority tribes: the Ekpeyes, Etches, Ikwerres, and the Ogonis (fig 8.2). While in the west, there are the Isokos.

There are four main languages spoken in the delta that correspond to the four main ethnics Ijaw, Isoko, Itsekiri and Urhobo. But Ijaw language has a multiplicity of dialects, such that almost every clan[1] has its own dialect with a similarity between them. By this we mean that, three or mores Ijaw from different clans (Ogboin, Opokuma, and Gbaran etc) can converse conveniently without problems of understanding each other.

---

[1]   The traditional classification of groups in Nigeria: Clan is a subdivision of tribe followed by city/town and town/village; quarter and finally family. (Tribe-> Clan-> City/Town-> Quarters-> Family).

However, in the delta region, kinship forms the essential part of the tribe, especially the clan rather than special relationship.

Despite the many clans, dialects and traditions, we can say they belong to the same cultural family. The people of the delta have many basic features in common. As well as various features of different groups of clans that make up the tribes[1] are the multiple facets of the same basic core.

However, the Ijaw have experienced as a separate group. From the linguistic point of view and from the perspective of time, it is very possible that the Ijo language[2] is without any link to others for at least five thousand years ago[3].

The difference in language suggests that allocation of the origin of Ijaw ethnic group to migration is unacceptable (or needs a deep research.). It is obvious that the Ijaws have lived as a group in the delta since centuries. Their power to adapt themselves to the difficult amphibious life and environment of the delta is a reason to believe it. The tradition of the Ijaws shows no place of origin except for the Niger Delta, but describes the migration and expansion within the delta (see supra—History of the settlement).

The Ijaws represent approximately 1.71 million people of the total official population of 3,590,000 h (1988). The eastern part of the Niger delta[4] with a low population density of 131.71 h/km² compared to Ikwerre and the Ogonis.

---

[1]   The Ijaw (Izon), the Urhobo, and Itsekiri.

[2]   Ijaw (Ijo), spellings that are used today, but the appropriate spelling is Izon because the alphabets in Ijo have no pronunciation for J, G, H, and ch or sh, so the J and G are pronounced Ze and Zi respectively, while ch and sh are Si.

[3]   Estimation by Dr Kay Williamson.

[4]   Part of the delta on which our study is focused. Bayelsa and Rivers States

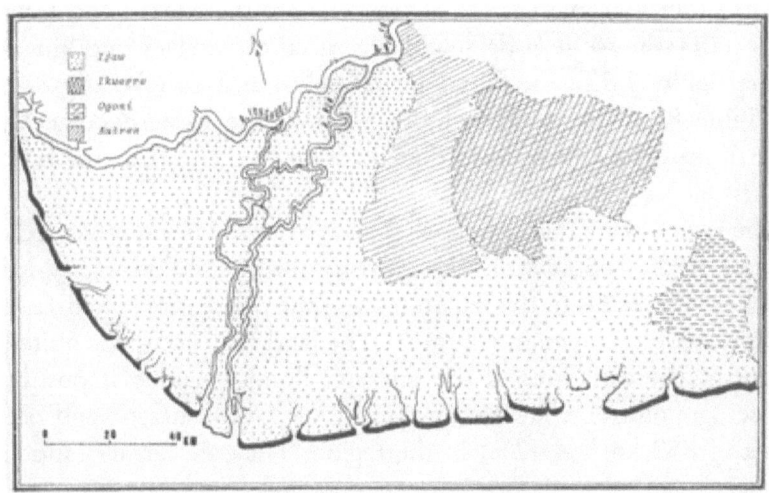

Fig 8.1: The main Ethnic groups in the Niger delta (East)

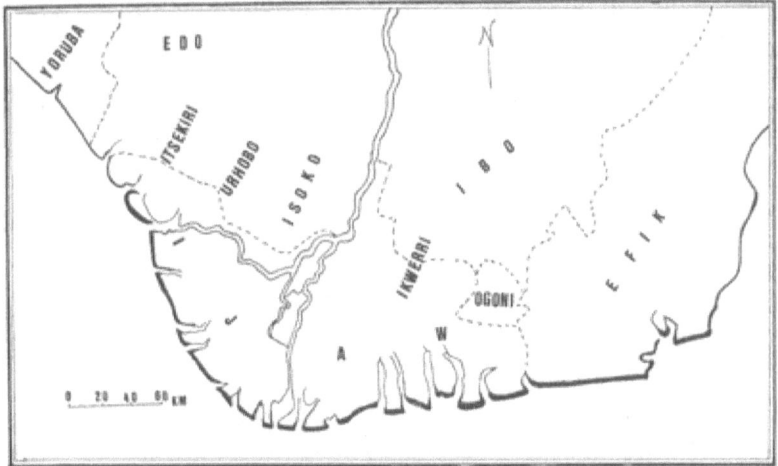

Fig 8.2: The cultural situation: The Ijaws and their neighbours in the Southern Nigeria.

So the density of the regional population in the same period is 184.90h/km². They occupy most of the land of the delta (Eastern part): About 67.05%. Most of them engage in commercial activities, transport and the craft industries. But the coastal Ijaw and the brackish water zone also do fishing, while those of fresh water also practice agriculture.

The other two main tribes of the delta are the Itsekiri and Urhobo. They occupy the western delta and organized themselves into kingdoms like the Benin (Edo), the kingdom of Itsekiri and Urhobo (fig 8.2 and 8.3). Table 8.1, summarizes the situation in the western delta. Other people of the delta, especially in the East (Our study area) are the Ikwerres and the Ogonis.

The Ikwerres are less numerous than the Ijaws. They represented only 10.5% of the total population with a density of 158.44 h/km². They occupy 2,980 km² (12.26%) in the region (east of the delta), the North-East (fig 8.1). The Ikwerre are mainly farmers. The land they occupy is quite high and out of the variations of the tide and floods, making it possible to practice agriculture. They have a density of 370.81 h/km² and occupy an area of 859 km² (4.42%) in the region. They are farmers and small traders.

Finally, the rest of the region (16.27%) is occupied by the minority tribes and represent 37.1% of the total population. They undertake, like their neighbours in one or the other of the activities mentioned above.

Fig 8.3: Districts of the Niger Delta (Western delta).

Lower Delta (South of Delta)	Upper Delta (North of Delta)
Ijaw (City States)	Aboh
Itsekiri	Isoko
	Urhobo

Table 8.1: The Kingdoms in the western Niger Delta

8.1.0. The Birth of Towns in the Niger Delta.

The birth or creation of towns in Nigeria could be divided into three periods:

(1) The pre-colonial towns (before 1900).
(2) The colonial towns (from 1900 to 1960).
(3) The post-colonial (from 1960-).

The Benin kingdom was a powerful and dominant kingdom in the south of Nigeria. It's then extended westward to Lagos, eastward to Bonny River and north wards to Idah. It was with them that the Portuguese established a diplomatic relations in their first visit to the Niger delta. The tradition of some people from the Niger delta shows that their ancestors came from the very kingdom of Benin to create their towns of today.

Indeed, the Oba (King) of Benin became very authoritarian and oppressive. This had resulted in the birth of the first towns in the delta. It should be noted that the concept of the birth of towns of delta itself, is applied from the arrival of migrants to the delta. This however does not include the Ijaw, who were already settled there in the delta.

The birth of the town of Brass is related to a battle lost by a General of the Benin army who was sent by the Oba (King) to go to end a rebellion on the outskirts of his empire. Unfortunately, he was defeated. It was a lost not only for the military, but also to the king; As a result, the General decided to settle with his men and Nembe was founded on the River Nun one of the main tributaries of River Niger. This town (Nembe) is considered the ancestral home by the "Brass men".

Obviously, the goal of the founders of towns in the delta was not only to escape the absolute monarchy of the Oba, but also to engage with the first settlers in fishing and the salt production[1]. These commodities have been requested by people from other parts of the country example the Igbos, the Edo etc. According to Pereira (1505), the people inside of delta were doing the exchange of yams, cow, goats and sheep for salt. However, it is clear that the reason for their migration to the delta was also for economic reasons.

Other towns were founded in the same ways while Port Harcourt was founded as a port by Mr D. L. Harcourt[2]. The city of Port Harcourt was fully established on the terminus of a railway to transport coal from the mines of Udi (Enugu). The land was subdivided in 1911 to Mr Harcourt. The construction of the city began in 1912 and was named after the name of the land owner, Mr Harcourt.

The delta towns were not created by the migrants from outside the Niger delta, but by the movements of individuals, following misunderstandings between brothers, and expulsion from the community etc. For example the founders of part of Okrika

(The part that speaks izon) and the village of Ikianbiri parted from Amassoma after misunderstanding and expulsion respectively.

All towns in the delta were founded or created by one way or the other of the above described processes—migration from outside the delta for economic, political or individual movements within the delta.

The end of the 16th century also marks the end of the processes of creating the city states. The Niger delta with the exception of some parts is occupied by the Ijaw, their language and traditions are distinct from their neighbours, the Igbo, the Ibibio, the Efik etc It is therefore clear that the birth of the city states is related to geographical, social and economic conditions (see history of settlement).

The active participation of Europeans on their arrival to the commercial activities[3] in the delta has contributed to the birth and development of the city states and the kingdoms. According to Olatunbosun (1981)

---

[1]   See infra—The activities of the inhabitants.

[2]   A British navigator from the Maritime department.

[3]   The coastal trade: the slave trade and natural products and the fight to control these businesses by the people of each town or city state transformed to an independent and individual state (city states).

that the birth of the city states in the delta was brought about by social conditions.

8.2.0. The first pre-colonial centres.

The Niger delta was not yet known in the history of settlement of Nigeria in the 13th century. The settlement itself has probably started after the creation of Benin Empire, although the Ijaw already lived there. Some people believed that their ancestors came from the Benin Empire. For example towards 1650, a son of the Oba of Benin based on delta, in the kingdom of Warri. Secondly, small states were formed, Brass, Bonny, the Ijaw and especially Kalabari (New Calabar).

In fact, the delta was inhabited by three distinct waves of migrations (Camara 1982). The oldest is that of Ijaw (Izon). Tradition assigns two sources for this population. First, is that they came from the north before the arrival of the Portuguese in the 15th century. The second, they could have come from the Kingdom of Benin from the 15th century fleeing the absolutism monasticism that was prevailing there.

These movements continued until the arrival of the British. This was increased by the commercial activities and the slave trade which marked the final wave of migration.

These different movements have resulted to the growth of the populations of the fishing villages in the Coastal Niger delta. As they continued to populate and develop, they became city states[1]. The kingdom of Itsekiri settled in the Niger delta (The western part of the delta) in the late 14th century around Warri city state. The tradition attests that initially the Itsekiri have been under the dominion of the kingdom of Benin. For the origin of the King of Itsekiri was from the Kingdom of Benin, a Prince called Iginua. In fact, the founder of Itsekiri tribe was Olua, the son of the King of Benin city, Prince Iginua. There are two versions about the migration of the Itsekiri. One is that the Prince Iginua (some write Ginuwa) was offered for sacrifice to the god of the river by his father in order to calm his anger against Benin City. He was found by Ijaw who asked him to stay with him (Ijaw) in Warri. The second version is that the jealousy of the other leaders for fears that the King's eldest son will not

---

[1] We define the city state, an autonomous city and have all the qualities of an independent sovereign state, a sovereign body irrespective of the type of his Government, they have a particular society individualized and personalized.

succeed him to the throne (King) after his death[1] and decided to found a kingdom in the delta. He was taken in a box and thrown into the river. He was taken by Ijaw (provisions were made by King Olua his father) to him was founded the Kingdom of Warri.

At first observation on the tradition of Ijaw in the entire delta, indicates that the central portion as the heart; other parts of which the city states were populated or created. Such as Ogobiri, Amassoma, Ikibiri, Oporoma, Opobo, Obiama inlet and in the central delta are the main centres of outward migration. Then, that of Oboloma and Ke (Nembe) in the eastern delta and Oporoza in the western part of the delta formed the secondary centres of migration (Alagoa 1984).

These migrations have resulted in the population growth of the fishing and small scale salt production (compared to that of the Atlantic trade) villages. The largest population movement[2] began between 1450 and 1800. This continued until the intervention of the slave trade that brought fundamental changes and transformed the societies of the delta communities.

In fact, the slave trade which reached its peak in 1865 leads to the birth of a class of intermediaries. If the slave trade depopulated the hinterland[3], it gives rise to highly centralized states, monarchical and oligarchic. They are centralized through a system of trading companies. The houses were both co-operative business and local Government, headed by the wealthy merchants. This was done with the participation more or less voluntarily hierarchical division of some slaves, bounded by a system of punishments and rewards. However, not the least promises of a lucrative commercial career. In addition, the Europeans introduced new articles of trade such as sea salt, serving slave trade ships coming from Bristol and Liverpool. And finally dried fish from Norway, clothing, metal tools, beads especially firearms. These were factors of considerable importance in that they

---

[1] Initially, the heads and the others sons of the King were jealous that Iginua be King after the death of their father. Secondly, Prince Iginua was considered the brain behind the oppressive acts and absolutism of the King. As a result, they do not want him to succeed their king after the death of their father.

[2] A distinction between the populations of migrants was not known until much later. Most likely in 1830 after the discovery of the coastal Niger Delta by the Europeans.

[3] Total of 370,000 were sold in twenty years to the slave traders (French Doc. N° 3151 on page 7).

allowed concentration in the hands of the few economic and political powers that favoured the settlement of the delta for example, the founder of Bonny, King Peple of Opobo.

From the 17th century, the Niger delta has become the most important commercial centre of slaves in West Africa. The inhabitants of the delta at that time were well established and took position as mediators of the trade. But the people of the coastal Niger Delta continued to increase due to the trafficking of slaves and natural resources that exist in the delta.

The direct contact within the country with the Europeans in the Nineteenth century had the monopoly of the coastal tribes brought an economic crises, political and social in the states of the Niger delta. In 1850, there were two commercial area in Nigeria, the Niger delta, the outlet of the Eastern Nigeria, the other being Lagos.

In the Niger delta, particularly at Bonny, the economy at that time had already been converted and was based on trade in the palm oil[1]. A campaign of 1855 to 1856 reported over 25,000 tons of palm oil from Bonny and Brass. Two hundred English houses were installed in the Niger Delta (The oil River) that exported regularly to Liverpool. Consular courts were installed at Bonny, Brass and Akassa in the Niger Delta.

By applying the international decision, the British Government has proclaimed on the 5th June 1885, the protectorate (Crowder 1962). The protectorate included the territories on the coast between the British Protectorate of Lagos and the right bank of the Rio Del Ray West (Cameroon). And the territories of the two banks of the Niger and its confluence with the Benue to the sea. Finally, the two banks of the Benue to Ibi, the confluence included.

These different types of trade in their nature promote migration and possible settlement in oil spots that gave the coast of the Niger delta its characteristic appearance of oil spot.

The coastal Niger Delta was completely unknown to the outside world, although the inhabitants of this region have already started commercial relationships with their neighbours including the Igbos, the Efiks. As a result, people with whom relationships have been established had their articles of trade and commerce limited. All of these were changed after two expeditions made by Mongo Park and the Lander brothers in search

---

[1]   The legal trade which replaced the slave trade.
     Curiosity or human, but the primary reason was economic, a change in the economy of the European continent.

of the courses of the Niger and Benue rivers which claimed the lives of many Europeans. How these two expeditions led to the discovery of the Niger Delta by the Europeans?

8.3.0. The discovery and exploration of the Coastal Niger Delta.

The coastal Niger Delta like many other countries and regions was unknown to the outside world although it was inhabited. The strong curiosity of the Europeans to know the source and the end of the Niger River led to the discovery of the Niger Delta. The course of the Niger River remained a mystery until 1830, when the first Europeans crossed the delta.

Several hypotheses have been given by several writers about the Niger River. But the general idea was that the Niger River had its source from the Atlas Mountains and ended in a lake. Then underground up to Abyssinia, and changes direction to the North and into the Mediterranean Sea on the course as the Nile. So, for several centuries, it was thought the Rivers Niger and the Nile was the same river. Alternately, according to other information sent by the Arab travellers that the Niger River is the same as the Senegal River. This was what J.C.H Ball believed in 1254. Why the exploration of the Niger River? The reasons were mainly on two reasons:

The first Europeans to cross the Niger delta were the Lander brothers, Richard and John in1830. Richard Lander was the servant of Clapperton during his second voyage in 1825. Arriving at Sokoto from Badagry, his Master fell ill and died in April 13, 1827. However, the only European survivor of these trips was Richard Lander. In 1830, the British Government sent Richard and John Lander (*two brothers*). At Bussa, King Yauri gave two canoes with men to lead them as far as to the mouth (estuaries) of the River Niger. They followed the river to the city of Onitsha, where they were captured by the Igbos. They were liberated by King Boy of Brass who led them to the coast. They returned to England on board a ship. It is this passage of the Lander brothers that solved the problems of the Niger River and the beginning of the knowledge and exploration of the Niger Delta by the Europeans.

The towns of the Niger Delta, at the arrival of the Europeans were all independent and individual. They were, however called the city states, considering the organization of their way of life and Government, such as the Ijaw lived in city states, while the Itsekiri formed Kingdoms. Why they

(Ijaw) lived in city states and the Itsekiri formed (living) kingdoms? The answers to these questions are related to the origins of their migration.

8.4.0. The Establishment of the British colonization.

During the period of the slave trade and the palm oil, the Kings or Paramount Chiefs had control of the rivers and creeks in the territories or the realms for example, Pepple of Bonny and Jaja of Opobo. European traders were limited to the coast with permission from the Kings. The contacts with the producers were by intermediaries. But in general, is the King who controls the estuaries of a river that also controls trade along the river. That said the policies of the delta were dominated by the power struggle to control trade in several interior environments and estuaries of rivers. The arrival of Europeans in the delta could probably due to the activities of European explorers, traders and missionaries. The explorers have mapped the rivers, creeks and made maps of the Delta. They were fascinated by the economic potentials of the region that attracted the attention of Europe.

The prohibition of the slave trade has not stopped trade relations between the Europeans and citizens of the delta. It was replaced par trade in palm oil. The Niger delta thus became the headquarters of the Nigerian economy. The urge to promote this new business led Britain into politics and possibly delta to the declaration of British protectorate in the region.

The Niger Delta provides experimental sites to practice the hopes of abolitionist "Trade school of Thought. Palm oil begins to make its effects by attracting British traders. For example, the city states of Bonny, the richest port became a pole of attraction to the British commercial and corporate imperialism. However, legitimate trade can not easily replace the slave trade. Bonny was a major slave trade operation port and felt the general effect of the sudden abrogation of the slave trade. The economy and the wealth of the Leaders were related to this inhuman and cruel trade. Despite the best efforts made by the British to frustrate the commerce (slave), some Europeans trafficked again this slave trade. However, between 1837 and 1854 British activities in the delta were to prevent the slave trade and to encourage the production of palm oil. The result was a conflict of interest. The British encouraged trade in palm oil while the supreme leaders and slave traders opposed to these intentions to discourage their inhuman profitable business. It is understood that these two types of trade can not co-exist.

In fact, a treaty was signed in 1837 with the supreme head of Bonny to protect British commercial interests. The treaty of 1838 removed all trust and other forms of processed confidence. However, the King had no more authority for punishment and justice. The effect of this treaty was to undermine (make the King less firm in these convictions and feelings) the King of Bonny. During the fifties the palm oil trade became more important and the African intermediaries in the Delta were now more profitable to practice.

Thus, in 1855-56 more than half of the total quantity of palm oil exported from Africa came from the Coastal Niger Delta. Bonny and New Calabar (Kalabari, an Ijaw clan) produced the largest quantities. The method of this trade was that the Europeans remained on board their ships while the intermediaries (coastal inhabitants) brought the palm oil inside. This allowed them to monopolize the trade. However, the Europeans (Liverpool Merchants) made more profit than the intermediaries, as the articles of the trade were used goods.

In 1854, a court of equity in order to minimize misunderstandings between European and African Traders was installed at Bonny. This court was composed of representatives of all the intermediaries of African and European merchants. Following the success, other courts were established in other city states in the delta.

Unfortunately, there were still misunderstandings between the Europeans merchants, who used the power of their local consulate to require intermediaries to accept their offer. British control of the oil rivers in the delta was established through the authority of the consular and diplomatic consulate.

A new page of Anglo-African relations was opened in 1849 following the appointment of John Beecroft to the Post of Consul of the Bights of Benin and Bonny (formally bight of Biafra). Consular activities consisted only of controls intermediaries in the policies of the delta and he urged the banner (Union Jack) to set up in any British territory occupied.

On the 15 February 1870, Jaja of Opobo declared the Kingdom of Opobo (sovereign) who was the largest state until the declaration of the British Protectorate of the oil river to its formal establishment. The final phase of British commercial activities in the delta marks the British administration of the region. After 1870, many Europeans countries were looking for territories in Africa, but the coastal Niger Delta was obtained by the British due to George Goldie Taubman who was called the founder of modern Nigeria. He unified the British Society of Niger Delta and prepared the statement of the Niger Delta Coast Protectorate in 1885. In 1900, most of what we called the coastal Niger Delta today went to the control of the British administration.

The economic strategies of the British government have resulted in the formation of the first city in the Niger Delta. The aim was to link the interior lines of communication with rail-road and road-river. This was the case of Port Harcourt (In 1912).

The city of Port Harcourt has easy access with all modern transport and with the roads. As a result, Port Harcourt serves as a hinge point of trade not only for the coastal Niger Delta, but for the whole country. A railway line was built, to link the coal mines in Enugu and Kaduna, transporting goods to Port Harcourt. Thus, the products manufactured imported from Europe arrive in the port of Port Harcourt.

In fact, the expansion of international economic relations in exportation of agricultural products, minerals and importation of manufactured products are huge attractions on the population of Port Harcourt. Consequently, Port Harcourt continues to exercise this right of attraction on all the infrastructure and therefore industrial and commercial activities. The proper functioning and viability of these authorities depends on a large labour force. However, increasing the concentration of these Economic activities is a real source of employment and better life. It is therefore not surprising that the concentration relevant to the urban population in Port Harcourt, and the attraction of rural populations (fig 1.2).

8.5.0. The traditional political organization

The origin of the creation and settlement of Nigerian cities was especially for defence and refuge, then trade. However, relief has played an important role in site selection for example Jos, Sokoto, Kaduna on the high plains; the highland of the west (Ogun, Oshun); the high mountains of the east (Enugu etc); the dense forest (the coastal Niger Delta) and so on.

The history of Nigeria begins long before the arrival of the Portuguese in the fifteenth century. Powerful Federal States have a remarkable system of government and whose term continues to impress and surprise even no contact yet seemed to have taken place with Europe. In the savannah saw the birth and development of the empire of Kanem-Bornu the Hausas. In the forest settled the Kingdom of Benin etc while in the coastal region of the Niger Delta has seen a host of village based social organizations. Their chief or King was known as Amananaowei or Amayanabo in Ijaw language. In the course of settlement of the Niger Delta, the locations (sites) occupied by the migrants were widely separated from each other. There were often Islands that dominate the communications to the inside. For example, the town of Bonny dominated the mouth of the river (estuary) that linked the interior from the Atlantic Ocean. In time, each community developed independence and individualism, a characteristic of the inhabitants of islands. However, each river mouth was a centre of commerce and in some cases each town has its Supreme Leader called Amananaowei and Amayanabo. Each city state (*This term is more appropriate than the term tribal-states, since migration had disrupted the links in the tribal system which has exacerbated by the slave trade*) had all the machinery of Government that allows them to maintain law and order, the administration of war and peace, to organize and continue the tranquillity of trade for centuries. In the first century, the delta states were grouped not only by royalty, but also contiguous (*attached to other Kings*). In the some period (*19th century*) citizenship became more by residence, and not by genealogy. The city-states are divided into two main political groups: the Kingdoms and the Republics. The main Kingdoms were Bonny (Iban), New Calabar (Kalabari), and Warri. The Republics in practice are units or commercial stations often with divided political authority, such as Old Calabar better illustrate the two political systems.

The Coastal Niger Delta

The Eastern Delta:
Tribes: Ijaw, Ikwerre, Ogoni, Ekpeye, Abua and others
Upper Delta (Northern Clans): Boma, Epiye-Atissa, Gbaran, Kolokuma, Ogbia, Ogboin.
Lower Delta (Southern Clans): Brass, Ibani, Kalabari, Nembe, Okrika.
Western Delta Tribes: Edo, Ijaw, Itsekiri, Isoko, Urhobo and others.

Table 8.2: The Social Organizations of the Niger delta Communities

In the modern coastal Niger Delta the classification of monarchy (Kingdom) and republic is also, almost over, but where it exists, are limited to traditional and cultural affairs only. As in other places the group classification is done by the ethnic presence. Ethnic groups: such as the Yoruba, Igbo, Hausa, Fulani, Edo, Ijaw, Efik etc. Then there are the sub-groups etc.

In the case of the coastal Niger delta, the classification (considering only large groups) Table 8.2 (1) shows the organization in reality it is much more complex, but we have shown only the most important of modern societies or communities of the delta. The tribe is the largest group representing an ethnic group at the National level. Tribe[1] are still sub-divided into sub-tribes (Clans), in the case of the eastern delta. The members of the same clan are often of the same genealogy[2], the same ancestors.

Their social life is organized mainly on the bases of family oriented attachment to individual freedom (boundless). The towns are again divided into compounds. Each compound is composed of brothers and their offspring of which, marriage between them is forbidden. Each of these Compounds considers themselves as members of the same family. Representatives of these compounds form the members of the chamber of

---

[1]   See the definition of the tribe above: the people of the delta, Chapter 8.
[2]   This division does not apply to all the tribes of the country; it applies in this case, only to an administrative division.

the King[1]. Although there are still the kings in some communities, their authorities are limited to traditional affairs or matters—traditional chiefs.

The City-States had contacts and trade links with one or the other by means of boats in the 15th century. They had trade relations with the Igbo and the Ibibio of the inter-land on fish, salt etc. This leads us to examine the population growth facilitated by these activities and commercial relations in the next chapter.

---

[1] Some of the clan-Heads (chiefs) are elected to represent their traditions in their States Government administration today.

Chapter 9

The population growth

The Coastal Niger Delta according to the 1963 census had a population of 1,768,032 inhabitants (Eastern Delta), ranking fifteenth among the states in Nigeria (21 States). It represented 3.18% of the total population of Nigerian. All data after 1963 are estimates or projections[1] until 2006. The population growth in the delta could be correctly analysed in two trenches: The first is Rivers State. This period will cover from 1963 to 1990. The second Rivers State and Bayelsa State separately, but as the Eastern delta and covers the period 1990 to 2006 (last valid census).

9.1.0. The general demographic trends.

The creation of States, the decentralization of public utilities and services by means of Local Authorities, Port development, industrial and commercial activities, led to a tremendous growth of the population of major cities and towns in the Niger Delta. This rapid growth was due partly to natural increase and partly to a new wave of immigration from all part of the country[2]. Most of them are the Igbo, Hausa and Ibibio in addition to the rural immigrants. For example, Port Harcourt, perhaps, because it is the only industrial city and the capital of the State, it has increased significantly due to immigration of youths of productive age in search of employment, for higher studies and so on. It is however, employment opportunities that make the difference between the rest of the Delta and

---

[1] The 2.5% used by Authorities of the delta, while 2.95% at national level.

[2] More precisely in late 1969 after the installation of the Government of Rivers State.

large populations, Port Harcourt etc were flooded with immigrants. The table shows the growth of the population of Port Harcourt and its suburbs, since 1963. As well as the nine other Local Government Authorities areas and their density per square kilometres (Appendices V).

In twenty years, from 1963 to 1983, the population of the delta (east) increased from 1,768,032 inhabitants to about 3,103,000 inhabitants (about 75% Increase). The Capital, Port Harcourt from 234,672 inhabitants to 574,000 inhabitants (+ 59% increase). And the population of the Delta increases to 3,772,000 inhabitants in 1990 (17% Increase) while that of Port Harcourt increased to 797,000 inhabitants (about 27%) in the same period. In fact, the only demographic data are from 1963 etc. which means that the populations are projections of those of 1963.

However, the divisions Administrative of the Local Government area have lost their significance and the people are higher then the projected population in the Niger Delta.

Indeed, the projections are calculated with an annual growth rate of 2.5% for rural areas and 5% for urban areas, Port Harcourt[1] etc *and the Niger Delta as a whole is considered a Rural Area*. However, increases in the general population in the study area from 1963 to 1990 table 8.3 are as follows:

Local Government Authority Area	Population	Population	1963-1983
	1963	1983	Increase %
Ahoada	179 329	298 233	66.30
Bonny	128 749	212 424	64.99
Bori	170 501	281 102	64.87
Brass	126 206	208 072	64.87
Degema	277 064	456 796	64.87
Ikwerre/Etche	201 849	332 790	64.87
Okrika/obibo/Tai-Eleme	163 629	269 776	64.87
Port Harcourt (Capital)	234 672	574 695	144.88
Sagbama	104 253	171 880	64.87

---

[1]   Composed of 1 to 18 electoral districts.

Yenagoa	181 770	299 502	64.81
TOTAL	1 768 032	3 105 350	75.64

Source: Population census of Nigeria 1963, eastern Nigeria
Vol. 1 and western Nigeria Vol.2; projections of 1983, 1990
A: Demographic trends from 1963-1983 in the 10 Local
Government Authority Areas

Local Government Authority Area	Population 1983	Population 1990	1983-1990 1983-1990
Ahoada	298 233	351 996	15.27
Bonny	212 424	252 706	15.94
Bori	281 102	334 656	16.00
Brass	208 072	247 710	16.00
Degema	456 796	543 815	16.00
Ikwerre/Etche	332 790	396 184	16.00
Okrika/obibo/ Tai-Eleme	269 776	321 171	16.00
Port Harcourt-Hq	574 695	797 337	27.92
Sagbama	171 880	204 627	16.00
Yenagoa	295 582	356 779	17.15
TOTAL	3 105 350	3 772 507	17.68

Source: Population census of Nigeria 1963, eastern Nigeria
Vol. 1 and western Nigeria Vol. 2; projections of 1983, 1990.
B: Demographic trends from 1983-1990 in the 10 Local
Government Authority Areas

Table 9.1: General demographic trends in the Niger Delta
(East of the Niger Delta)

Table 9.1 shows that from 1963 to 1983 an average increase of about
73% of the total population of the ten Local Authority Areas. The only
area of Port Harcourt has an increase of more than about 144%, followed
by the area of Ahoada. While, the overall increase in the region is about
75%. However, in 1990, the Local Government Authority Area of Yenagoa
had the highest growth (17%) compared to other areas of LGAs.

To determine the origin of the population growth of the cities/towns in the Delta, one must first of all highlights the mobility of the rural population. But since the length of the calculation method required, we can cite only a few examples (table 9.3) for Amassoma. From the documents of the 1963 census and 1990 estimations of the general population, shows that the Municipal population of Amassoma was 19,383 inhabitants in 1963, while that of 1990 (*Projection of 1963 census*) about 38,000 inhabitants. The growth is about 18,000. It is impossible, based on the documents in our disposal to give more details about the new arrivals and distances exceeding the total natural and new populations. However, this was a population that had undergone a relatively shape increase, as it increased by more than 46% from 1963 to 1986 and about 9% from 1986 to 1990 (Table 9.3) for the towns.

N°	Town/City	Population 1963	Population 1990	1963-1990	Increase %
1	Ahoada	6329	12 423	6 094	49.05
2	Ofoni-Agbanga	6 236	12 240	6 004	49.05
3	Ohalimini	4 071	7 990	385	49.05
4	Kugbo	3 667	7198	3 703	49.06
5	Agbere	3 495	6 860	3 365	49.05
6	Erema	3 013	5913	2 901	49.04
7	Emelego	2 915	5 772	2 807	49.49
8	Edeoha	2 716	5 331	2615	49.05
9	Obuburu-Obigbo	2 490	4 888	2 398	49.06
10	Mgbede	2 459	4827	2 368	49.06
11	Egbem-Okwuzu	2 395	4 700	2 305	49.04
12	Alinso-Okanu	2 207	4 332	2 125	49.05
13	Ihiukwu	2 172	4 263	2 091	49.05
14	Idu-Obusuiku	2 076	4.074	1 998	49.04
15	Ndoni	2 038	4.000	1962	49.05
16	Akabuka-Ibewa	2 000	3 925	1 925	29.04
17	Ogbogu	1 752	3 439	1687	49.05
18	Umuanya	1 723	3 382	1659	49.05
19	Adoda	1 711	3 358	1647	49.05
20	Eziaga	1 705	3 278	1 573	47.99
21	Emilaghan	1 670	3 346	1 676	50.09
22	Umunkaru	1 612	3 164	1552	49.05
23	Okarki	1 605	3 150	1 545	49.05
24	Odoni	1 568	3 077	1 509	49.04
25	Ogbo	1 562	3 066	1 504	49.05
26	Umuebe-Obieti	1 550	3 042	1 492	49.05
27	Orupata	1 500	2 944	1 444	49.05

(a) Ahoada local Government Authority area.

N°	Town/City	Population 1963	Population 1990	1963-1990	Growth %
1	Opobo	34 458	69 597	34 139	50.49
2	Ngo-Town	8 073	15 846	7 773	49.05
3	Bonny Town	7 410	14 543	7133	49.05
4	Nkoro Main Town	4 557	8 944	4 387	49.05
5	Ataba Town	4 125	8 096	3 971	49.05
6	Isila Ogono	3 841	7 539	3 698	49.05
7	Asarama	3 538	6 945	3 407	49.05
8	Agwat Ubong	3 050	5 986	2 936	49.05
9	Okorolo	2 588	5 080	2 492	49.06
10	Olotumbi	2 235	4 386	2 151	49.04
11	Nanabie	2 107	4 135	2 028	49.04
12	Etekan Unyeada	1 894	3 717	1 823	49.04
13	Nyama Agama	1 763	3 461	1696	49.06
14	Okama-Ekede Odidin	1 650	3 239	1 589	49.06
15	Iwokiri	1565	3 072	1 507	49.07
16	OtuoOgbolo Akong	1 546	3034	1488	49.04
17	Bema	1 524	2 991	1 467	49.05
18	Kalaibiama	1 508	2 960	1 452	49.05

(b) Bonny Local Government Authority

N°	Town/City	Population 1963	Population 1990	1963-1990	Increase %
1	Bodo	14 257	27 983	13 726	49.05
2	Kegbara Dere	10 326	20 255	9 929	49.02
3	Bomu	9 504	18 643	9 139	49.02
4	Bori	9 163	17 985	8 822	49.05
5	Yeghe	7 663	15 041	7 378	49.05
6	Baranyonwa Dere	6 976	13 681	6 708	49.01
7	Sii	4 503	8 839	4 336	49.06
8	Biara	4 240	8 322	4 082	49.06
9	Bera	4 123	8 093	3 970	49.05
10	Mogho	3 604	7 070	3 466	49.02
11	Beeri	3 500	6 870	3 370	49.05
12	Okwali	3 224	6 328	3 104	49.05
13	Nweo/Nweol	3 144	6 167	3 023	49.02
14	Kono Boue	2 828	5 550	2 722	49.05
15	Opuoko	2 588	5 079	2 491	49.05
16	Bere	2 576	5 056	2 480	49.05
17	Lewe	2 508	4 920	2 412	49.02
18	Bean	2 434	4 777	2 343	49.04
19	Deyor	2 424	4 758	2 334	49.05
20	Luckwe Bangha	2 418	4 746	2 328	49.05
21	Kpean	2 364	4 640	2 276	49.05
22	Kono	2 061	4 045	1 984	49.05
23	Lori	2 012	3 949	1 934	48.49
24	Luyorgwaro	2 002	3 929	1 927	49.05
25	Wiyakara	1 991	3 908	1 917	49.05
26	Jor Sogho	1 938	3 804	1 866	49.05
27	Kabangha	1 909	3 747	1 838	49.05
28	Taabaa	1 909	3 747	1 838	49.05
29	Barako	1 821	3 574	1 753	49.05
30	Duburo	1 789	3 511	1 722	49.05
31	Eken	1 736	3 407	1 671	49.05

32	Buan	1 588	3 117	1 529	49.05
33	Kpor	1 587	3 113	1 526	49.02
34	Luawi	1 580	3 101	1 521	49.05
35	Lumene Bangha	1 563	3 068	1 505	49.05
36	Kpong	1 506	2 956	1 450	48.38

(c) Bori Local Government Authority Area.

N°	Town/City	Population 1963	Population 1990	1963-1990	Increase %
1	Nembe	23 626	46 372	22 746	49.05
2	Akassa	4 913	9 641	4 728	49.04
3	Kolo	4 802	9 426	4 624	49.07
4	Okpoma	4 385	8 607	4 222	49.05
5	Oloibiri	3 376	6 626	3 250	49.05
6	Okoroba	3 292	6 461	3 169	49.05
7	Anyama	3 260	6 398	3 138	49.05
8	Idema	3 053	5 993	2 940	49.05
9	Emeyal	3 014	5916	2 902	49.05
10	Opomatobo	2 883	5 659	2776	49.05
11	Okodogu	2 762	5 421	2 659	49.05
12	Ibelebiri	2 683	5 272	2 589	49.11
13	Otuokpoti	2 592	5 087	2 495	49.05
14	Egbedama	2 436	4781	2 345	49.05
15	Odobio	2 312	4 538	2 226	49.05
16	Ogidiama	2 250	4 416	2 166	49.05
17	Imiringi	2 157	4 234	2 077	49.06
18	Odiama	1 913	3 755	1 842	49.05
19	Atubo	1 876	3 682	1 806	49.05
20	Otuaka	1 848	3 627	1 779	49.05
21	Akipelai	1 809	3 551	1 742	49.06
22	Fantuo	1 805	3 543	1 738	49.05
23	Akalabage	1 804	3 541	1 737	49.05
24	Okokokiri	1 715	3 366	1 651	49.05
25	Brass	1 616	3 172	1 556	49.05

(d) Brass Local Government Authority Area.

N°	Town/City	Population 1963	Population 1990	1963-1990	Increase %
1	Buguma	100 628	197 509	97 881	49.56
2	Abonnema	53 261	104 539	51 278	49.05
3	Bakana	29 592	55 980	26 388	47.14
4	Tombia	16 462	32 311	15 849	49.05
5	Ido	7 407	14 539	7 132	49.05
6	Kula	7 193	14 118	6 925	49.05
7	Opu Degema	7 192	14 116	6 924	49.05
8	Buguma	6 246	12260	6 014	49.05
9	Bille	4 854	6 528	4 674	25.64
10	Obonoma	4 077	8 003	3 926	49.06
11	Isoko	3 681	7 225	3 544	49.05
12	Kala-Degema	3 621	7 107	3 486	49.05
13	Abalama	3 332	6 540	3 208	49.05
14	Obuama	3 249	6 377	3 128	49.05
15	Oke	2 067	4 058	1 991	49.06
16	Oporoma	2 055	4 033	1 978	49.05
17	Krakrama	1 830	3 592	1 762	49.05
18	Angulama	1 682	3 301	1619	49.05
19	Old Bakana	1 620	3 179	1 559	49.04

(e) Degema Local Government Authority Area.

N°	Town/City	Population 1963	Population 1990	1963-1990	Increase %
1	Elele	10 560	20 727	10167	49.05
2	Omanelu	7 135	14 005	6 870	49.05
3	Isiokpo	6 515	12 788	6 273	49.05
4	Egbeda	6 473	12 705	6 232	49.05
5	Umudioga	6 013	11 802	5 789	49.05
6	Igwuruta	5 264	10 332	5 068	49.05
7	Ibaa	5 132	10 072	4 941	49.06
8	Ubima	4 980	9 775	4 795	49.05
9	Elele Alimini	4 864	9 547	4 683	49.05
10	Omagwa	4 395	8 627	4 332	50.21
11	Aluu	4 333	8 505	4 172	49.05
12	Abelle	4 305	8 450	4 145	49.05
13	Apani	4 056	7 961	3 905	49.05
14	Umuogba	4 009	7 869	3 860	49.05
15	Odagwa	3 643	7 151	3 508	49.06
16	Ulakwo	3 574	7 015	3 441	49.05
17	Igbodo	3 460	6 791	3 331	49.05
18	Umnoye	3 246	6 371	3 125	49.05
19	Rumuji	3 180	6 242	3 062	49.05
20	Umuechem	2 856	5 606	2 750	49.05
21	Ndele	2 720	5 339	2 619	49.05
22	Ubimini	2 703	5 306	2 603	49.06
23	Oduoha	2 698	5 295	2 597	49.05
24	Okeki	2 698	5 278	2 589	49.05
25	Ndashi	2 671	5 243	2 572	49.06
26	Umuanwa	2 618	5 139	2 521	49.06
27	Obidi	2 614	5 130	2 516	48.07
28	Egbu	2 562	5 028	2 466	49.05
29	Chokocho	2 519	4 944	2 425	49.05
30	Ozuzu	2 395	4 700	2 305	49.04
31	Igbo-Etche	2 372	4 655	2 283	49.04

32	Mba	2 315	4 544	2 229	49.05
33	Rumuoro	2 258	4 432	2 174	49.05
34	Akwa	2 125	4 192	2 074	49.48
35	Omuadaeme	2 138	4 171	2 033	48.74
36	Igwururuta-Ali	2 094	4 110	2 016	49.05
37	Rumuewhor	2 013	3 951	1 938	49.05
38	Umuajuloke	2 010	3 945	1 935	49.05
39	Rumuche	1 979	3 884	1905	49.05
40	Rumuodogo	1 967	3 861	1 894	49.05
41	Okporowo	1 938	3 804	1 866	49.05
42	Umubulu	1 912	3 753	1 841	49.05
43	Ozuoha	1 902	3 733	1831	49.05
44	Afara	1 833	3 597	1 764	49.04
45	Egwi	1 729	3 394	1 665	49.06
46	Obite	1 624	3 188	1 564	49.06
47	Umudikomo	1 617	3 174	1 557	49.05
48	Umunwengi	1 515	2 973	1 458	49.02

(f) Ikwerre/Itche Local Government Authority Area

N°	Town/City	Population 1963	Population 1990	1963-1990	Increase %
1	Okrika Island	24 138	47 378	23 240	49.05
2	Ogun	14 000	27 479	13 479	49.05
3	Kani	7 343	14 412	7 069	49.05
4	Ogoloma	6 329	12 423	6 094	49.05
5	Oyigbo	6 020	11 816	5 796	49.05
6	Ebubu	4 539	8 909	4 370	49.05
7	Alesa	4 427	8 690	4 263	49.06
8	Obeama	3 974	7 800	3 826	49.05
9	Akpajo	3 861	7 578	3 717	49.05
10	Aleto	3 775	7 409	3 634	49.05
11	Agbonchia	3 331	6 538	3 207	49.05
12	Ban-Ogoyi	3 157	6 157	3 000	48.73
13	Nonwa-Kenbara	3 077	6 039	2 962	49.05
14	Bolo	2 965	5 819	2 854	49.05
15	Onne	2 705	5 309	2 604	49.05
16	Ogale	2 540	4 985	2 445	49.05
17	Kom-Kom	2 440	4 789	2 349	49.05
18	Bamu	2 419	4 749	2 329	49.04
19	Kpuite	2 165	4 250	2 085	49.06
20	Ibaka	2 111	4 144	2 033	49.06
21	Botem	2 030	3 984	1 954	49.05
22	Nonwa Uedume	1 952	3 832	1 880	49.06
23	Umuagbai	1 856	3 643	1 787	49.05
24	Alode	1 800	3 533	1 733	49.05
25	Abote	1 699	3 335	1 636	49.06
26	Kalio	1 680	3 298	1 618	49.06
27	Okoroma	1 556	3 054	1 498	49.05

(g) Okrika/Oyigbo/Tai Local Government Authority Area.

N°	Town/City	Population 1963	Population 1990	1963-1990	Increase %
1	Port Harcourt	175 570	675 603	500 033	74.01
2	Rumuokurushie	7 363	14 452	7 089	49.05
3	Rumuomasi	5 220	10 246	5 026	49.05
4	Rumuobiakani	4 419	8 674	4 255	49.05
5	Elelenwo	3 616	7 097	3 481	49.05
6	Eneka	2 768	5 433	2 665	49.05
7	Iriebe	2 689	5 278	2 589	49.05
8	Rumuokwuta	2 159	4 300	2 141	49.79
9	Rumueme	1 875	3 680	1 805	49.05
10	Rumuegbo	1 868	3 667	1 799	49.06
11	Rumuolumeni	1759	3 452	1 693	49.04
12	Abuloma	1 752	3 439	1 687	49.05
13	Choba	1 746	3 427	1 681	49.05
14	Nkpoku	1692	3 321	1 627	49.05
15	Ogbogoro	1 660	3 257	1 597	49.03
16	Oroigwe	1 618	3 176	1 558	49.06
17	Rumogba	1 502	2 948	1 446	49.05

(h) Port Harcourt Local Government Authority Area

N°	Town/City	Population 1963	Population 1990	1963-1990	Increase %
1	Aleibiri	7 706	15 125	7 419	49.05
2	Ofoni	6 236	12 240	6 004	49.05
3	Pertorugbene	6 195	12 160	5 965	49.05
4	Ndoro (I &II)	6 058	11891	5 833	49.05
5	Ekeremor	6 038	11 851	5 813	49.05
6	Ossiama	4 773	9 368	4 595	49.05
7	Agbobiri	3 660	7 184	3 524	49.05
8	Agbere	3 495	6 860	3 365	49.05
9	Angalabiri	3 388	6 649	3 261	49.04
10	Isampou	3 317	6 511	3 194	49.06
11	Trofani	2 935	5 761	2 826	49.05
12	Ebedebiri	2 864	5 622	2 758	49.06
13	Tungbo	2 807	5 509	2 702	48.87
14	Akede	2 652	5 205	2 553	49.05
15	Sagbama	2 380	4 671	2 291	49.05
16	Kabiama	2 236	4 388	2 152	49.02
17	Anyamasa	1 968	3 863	1 895	49.06
18	Adagbabiri	1 924	3 776	1 852	49.05
19	Ikpidiama	1 718	3 373	1 655	49.07
20	Bolo-Orua	1 707	3 350	1 643	49.04
21	Toru-Angiama	1 643	3 224	1 581	49.04
22	Toru-Ibeni	1 599	3 138	1 539	49.04
23	Odoni	1 568	3 077	1 509	49.04

(i) Sagbama Local Government Authority Area.

N°	Town/City	Population 1963	Population 1990	1963-1990	Increase %
1	Amassoma	19 383	38 790	19 407	50.03
2	Odi	13 587	26 669	13 082	49.05
3	Otuan	11 635	22 836	11 201	49.05
4	Igbomatoru	5 322	10 446	5 124	49.05
5	Ekowe	4 921	9 658	4 737	49.05
6	Okoloba	4 031	7 912	3 881	49.05
7	Kaiama	3 576	7 019	3 443	49.05
8	Sabagreia	3 385	6 644	3 259	49.05
9	Oporoma	3 365	6 605	3 240	49.05
10	Igbedi	3 328	6 532	3 204	49.05
11	Ikibiri	3 019	5 926	2 907	49.06
12	Peremabiri	2 862	5 618	2 756	49.06
13	Aguobiri	2 864	5 268	2 584	49.05
14	Korokorosei	2 593	5 089	2 496	49.05
15	Ikebiri	2 450	4 809	2 359	49.05
16	Enewari	2 370	4 652	2 282	49.05
17	Tein (I&II)	2 241	4 399	2 158	49.06
18	Kpansia	2 211	4 340	2 129	49.84
19	Amatolo	2 131	4 194	2 063	49.19
20	Opuama	1 909	3 747	1 838	49.05
21	Igbogene	1 861	3 653	1 792	49.06
22	Olugbobiri	1 844	3 619	1 775	49.05
23	Azuzuama	1 804	3 541	1 737	49.05
24	Tombia	1 754	3 443	1 689	49.06
25	Okolobiri	1 732	3 400	1 668	49.06
26	Agudama-Epie	1 723	3 382	1659	49.05
27	Ogboloma	1 721	3 378	1 657	49.05
28	Bomadi	1 709	3 355	1 646	49.06
29	Yenizue-Opu	1698	3 333	1 635	49.05
30	Angiama	1 635	3 210	1 575	49.07
31	Yenagoa	1 608	3 156	1548	49.05

32	Okowari	1 587	3 115	1 528	49.05
33	Fangbe	1 561	3 064	1 503	49.05
34	Polaku	1 528	3 000	1 472	49.07

(j) Yenagoa Local Government Authority Area.

Table 9.2: The Demographic trends of all populations of the Towns /City of 1 500 and more inhabitants in 1963 Census.

The Fig 9.1 expresses the results of 1963 census. This map does show only the administrative areas of the Local Governments, and not the towns as basic unit. This is because the towns are generally a very small area, would have made small patches on the map. On the other hand, we have not available maps that give the outlines of the towns or the means to establish ourselves.

This map is not intended to give limited information, because it includes only the towns and villages that were identifiable by cartographic localization (aerial photographs). It is characteristic that in the delta, towns on the map can actually group several villages or towns, for example Okrika, Ogbia, Nembe, Akassa . . . As against the census results are included in each town/city or village. However, we have no detailed maps of the districts to establish more detailed map of the distribution of densities. These are not available to us at the moment, but hope to obtain then in the future.

Administrative Division	Census 1963	Projection 1990	Growth 1963-1990	Growth %
Oporoma (5 Towns/Villages)	8 571	17 154	8 583	50,03
Tarakiri (5 Communities)	3 915	7 835	3 920	50,03
Otuan	11 635	23 284	11 649	50,03
Olodiama (6 Communities)	9 008	18 028	9 020	50,03
West Boma (6 Communities)	5 726	11 460	5 734	50,03

Central Boma (4 Communities)	9 617	19 247	9 630	50,03
Amassoma	19 383	38 790	19 407	50,03
East Boma (13 Communities)	9 262	18 534	9 272	50,03

Source: Population Census of Nigeria 1963 (Vol. I (Eastern Region), Vol. II (Western Region)

Table 9.3: The localization and origin of growth according to the electoral Constituency in the District of Oporoma

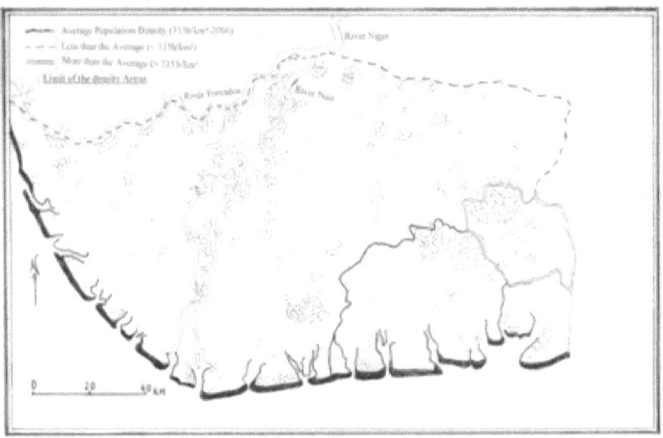

A point represents 250 people.

Fig. 9.1: The distribution and density of Population in the study area (Census 2006)

Nevertheless, we have represented on this map, cities and towns/villages of 3000 inhabitants or more, and at least 80% of those less than 3000 habitants. A point on the map represents 250 people. It occupies the site of the towns and villages and is not uniformly distributed within the territory of the towns. The map reflects obviously the density map. It shows the appearance along the Nun river almost continues series of towns and villages and discontinues or broken on the Forcados river. These spread over the entire northern part of the delta towards the ocean (south). On the other hand the North East covered by large and medium towns that do not disappear in hundreds of areas to the east (The river Nun)-west. Unlike the southern part, small towns occupy lowlands around some areas of towns of 15,000 inhabitants. The average density is about 91 people per square kilometres (fig 9.1).

9.1.0. The recent growth of the urban population

The urban growth in the coastal Niger Delta has been fostered by all the geographic and economic factors. Since the arrival of Europeans, these factors have contributed to the creation of the urban areas, especially Port Harcourt region etc.

9.1.1. The global growth and urban expansion

Nigerian demographic data (table 9.3 and 9.4) in 1930 to 1950 are simply compilations of existing documents. But a census was conducted in 1952 in the west in December 1952 and in June 1953 (East), while that of 1963 was conducted in November1963 throughout the country. Tables 9.3 and 9.4 summarize the situation of urban populations throughout the country and the coastal Niger Delta based on the census of 1963.

The tables evoke growth phenomenon of urban populations. Table 9.3 discusses two growth periods: the colonial period from 1930 to 1960 and Post-colonial period (graphic 9.1). The urban population growth during the colonial period was probably due to the policy pursued by the British administration in terms of social facilities. In addition, the social facilities provided by the colonial administration have contributed to the decrease in mortality and improved the living conditions. This has given an official growth rate of 2.00%. These facilities were concentrated in the urban centres. However, their growth rate were higher (5.00%) compared to rural areas.

During the Post-Colonial period (from 1960), these social facilities have been multiplied, since the country was divided into three regions: North, East and West so a better distribution of the social facilities. (Tables 9.1; 9.2 and Graph 9.1; 9.2) show the percentage increase of urban population of Nigeria and that of the Coastal Niger Delta (Eastern). But the concentration of the urban population lived in the area we now call Port Harcourt and its suburbs. However, there were towns like Bonny,

Buguma, Okrika, Amassoma etc that have populations of over 36,000 inhabitants.[1]

Nigeria				The Coastal Niger Delta (East)		
Year	Total	Urban	pop	Total	Urban	Pop
	pop	Absolute	%	Pop	Absolute	%
1930	24 645 275	1 581 255.22	6.42	666 594	79 860	11.98
1940	31 548 035	2 575 699.11	8.16	895 847	112 650	12.57
1950	40 384 152	4 195 542.44	10.39	1 203 944	158 904	13.20
1960	51 695 129	6 834 096.53	13.22	1 618 000	224 150	13.85
1970	66 174 136	11 132 023.13	16.82	2 180 497	365 117	16.74
1980	84 708 489	18 132 892.65	21.41	2 942 042	594 737	20.22
1990	109 491 920	29 536 571.41	26.98	3 979 730	954 925.16	23.99

Source: Annual abstracts of statistics Federal Office of statistics

Lagos 19   Pop = Population

Table 9.4: The size of the urban population from 1930-1990

	Nigeria		The Coastal Niger Delta (East)	
	Total Population	Urban Population	Total Population	Urban Population
1930-1940	28.01%	62.89%	34.39%	41.06
1940-1950	28.01%	62.89%	34.39%	41.06%
1950-1960	28.01%	63.60%	34.39%	41.06%
1960-1970	28.20%	62.89%	34.76%	62.89%
1970-1980	28.01%	62.89%	34.93%	62.89%
1980-1990	22.63%	38.61%	26.07%	60.54%

Same source: Federal Office of statistics.

Table 9.5: Urban population Growth

---

[1]   The series of towns and villages could have continued as the river Nun, if we pushed the limits (west) of our study by about a kilometre.

Population		Growth	Population		Growth	Population		Growth
1963	1983	%	1983	1990	%	1990	2006	%
1 768 032	3 105 350	75.64	3 105 350	3 772 507	17.68	3 772 507	6 888 758	45.00

Table 9.6: The demographic Evolution of the Eastern Niger Delta from 1963 to 2006

This table shows three unique phases of population growth:

(a) From 1963-1983 [20 yrs]; this period includes migrations due to the creation of Rivers State. The Delta citizens that were living in other States in the country return back home with the feeling of belonging now to a State, to a State of their own, which explains the brutal demographic rise in the Eastern Niger Delta.

(b). From 1983-1990 [7 yrs]; this phase explains the tendency to stability (delta citizens), except migrants from other State citizens. Though the period is short but it explains the principle.

(c) From 1990-2006 [16 yrs]. This period includes the creation of Bayelsa State (1996). Though more than 50% of the migrants came from within the Delta, and more than 30% of the Delta people still return home from other States of the country. The rest citizens are from other States as businessmen, traders etc.

Though, we did not use the same interval (20, 7, 16 yrs) for our analysis, but the periods considered represent high, normal and low demographic growth necessary to make planning programs.

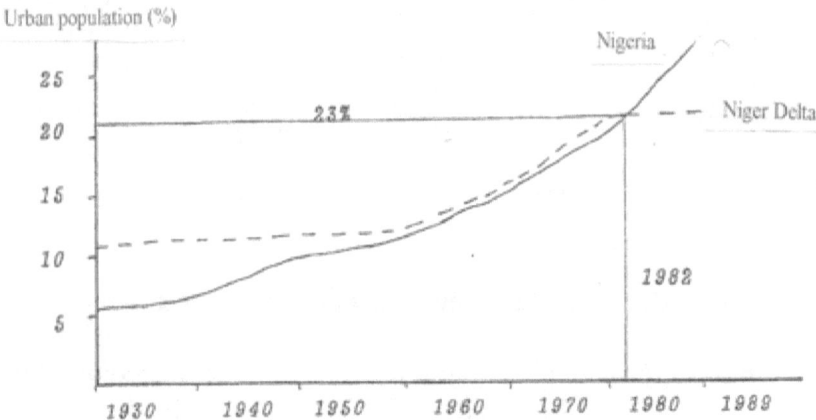

Graph 9.1: The evolution of the urban population
(1930-1989) of the delta compared to that of the country.

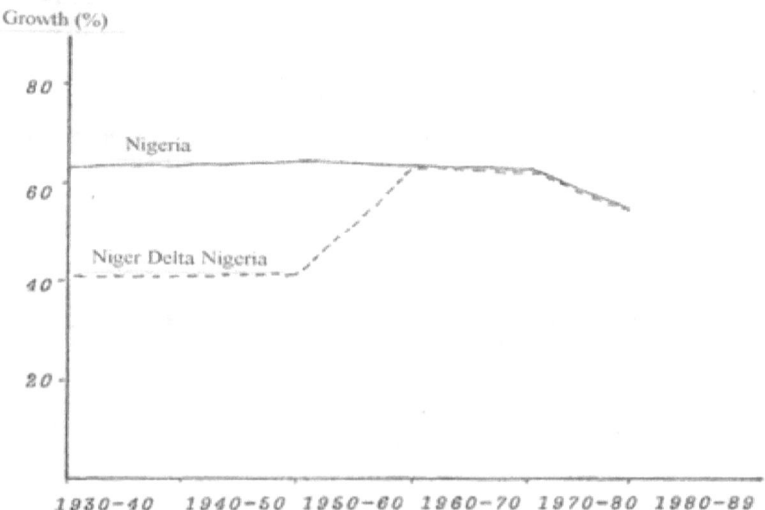

Graph 9.2: The evolution of the urban population growth in
the delta

In fact, the wave of the recent growth of the urban population
was from 1960 onwards. In 1963, the Nigerian urban population was
7,911,321 inhabitants, representing 14.21% of the total population. In
addition, this represented a population that lived in 90 towns classified as

urban. In this urban population of the Country, the Coastal Niger Delta represented only 3.28% (259,482 h) with four urban centres. However, the urban population as percentage of the total population was only 16.80%. It should be noted that the official rate of the population growth increased from 2.00% to 2.5%, while that of the urban population was 5.00%. As a result, some private estimates have used rates ranging from 2.8% to 3.5%. This has resulted in the differences observed between the Nigerian population projections by different Agencies: for example, "Jeune Afrique magazine" used 2.6% as growth rate from 1970 to 1977.

The evolution of the urban population in the Coastal Niger Delta seems brutal, because the number of towns classified as urban in 1963 was four. This number increased to 18, including Port Harcourt and the towns of 20,000 inhabitants or more. Two of these towns have more than 99,000 inhabitants: Abonnema (99,502 h) and Buguma (187,992 h) while Port Harcourt with over 600,000 inhabitants. Finally, 35 towns have more than 5,000 inhabitants (1988 estimates).

In fact, the urban character of the towns in the coastal Niger Delta is not the result of industrial activities, but trade and administrative services. Port Harcourt has as well as industrial activities and intellectual which gives its diversity, its personality and attractiveness. It is however, no wonder rapid growth of the urban population of the Port Harcourt Local Government Authority Area. The criteria of determination and classification of urban areas remains the sole responsibility of the Governor of the State. The Governor in accordance with Act N° 6 of 1978 relating to land use decisions and could appoint a settlement such as an urban population[1]. Thus, an urban population can only count 3,004 inhabitants (Yenagoa). The distinction between urban and rural areas in the Coastal Niger Delta does not reflect reality. It is therefore necessary to revise that notion and the classification criteria for determining urban centres[2] for the Niger Delta.

In fact, among the few indisputably urban population groups which are defined as much by their functions and populations (Table 11.1) and rural areas that are not agricultural areas are also growing parts. This might be called the semi-urban areas. This intermediate category as we call it

---

[1]   Throughout the country, the statistical definition of an urban population is a population of 2,000 inhabitants or more. But the Niger Delta (East) seems to be a special case.

[2]   The status of an urban population.

(2,500 habitants) having no radiation areas. Majority of this category of population is situated in the southern part of the Niger Delta. And many groups of the populations are fishermen and alcohol producers. However, urban and rural frontiers once seemed immutable. Those of the semi-urban are constantly modified by the crossing of population or by structural changes (e g. Kaiama). In terms of population growth and structural change, it seems that these boundaries are tending to be disappearing. These are through the interpenetration of increasingly and frequently appearing three categories of populations in the complex economic and socially exceeding the local framework that characterize them. Although some historic towns such as Bonny, Brass, Port Harcourt, Ahoada etc are known for centuries, the towns in the delta were still considered fishing villages. This was designed by the Government Authorities since the time of the Administration of the Eastern Region[1]. For example in 1967 just before the creation of the Rivers State, the Secretary General of the then Yenagoa Province nicknamed 'The Ojukwu of Yenagoa' *(In a way the Governor of the Province)* made a speech after his first official visit around the province said, "the Niger Delta is not only made up of villages and fishing ports, but also cities and towns." And then, promised giving true image of the Niger Delta to Government. The creation of River State in the Niger Delta in 1967 marks a turning point in the history of the Niger Delta, eventually, the recognition and redefinition and reclassification of its towns and villages.

As a result, towns like Amassoma, Odi, and Kaiama etc were reclassified as big towns. But the social facilities and projects for these towns were far from being integrated into the programs of the Government authorities (Eastern Region). Indeed, the growth of economic activities of these towns influence the nearby towns and villages especially those non-agricultural (-30% average) for development of trade, craft, river transport and so on. In particularly Amassoma, Buguma, Abonnema.

The civil war (Biafra) that began July 6, 1967 has changed the Nigerian society (Appendices I). The four Regions were divided into 12 States, then into 19 States and to 21 in 1988, but today (2011) 36 states (1996) in the country. Minorities, once dominated by the majority ethnic groups assert their will to play a role. They have become masters at least at home. Each and every one of them became conscious of their delay in all fields

---

[1]   When Nigeria had three Regions (North, East and West) and then 4 (+ Mid-West).

of development, try now to snatch from the Federal responsibilities: the industry or appropriation to enable them to meet some of their disabilities (lacking).

In the Coastal Niger Delta, the war has set an obstacle to the growth and development of its towns. The creation of Rivers State (East of the Delta) has given hope that finally, part of the delta could now be developed and possibly urbanization and extension of its towns. But unfortunately the creation of this State was followed by the declaration of the republic of Biafra by the secessionist forces from the Eastern Region of the country. Although, initially business continued, but later almost all activities came to a halt, except renovation of homes destroyed by natural causes. This continued until the end of the civil war in 1970.

Nevertheless, not all areas of the delta had much destruction by the civil war except the North of the delta, the areas where the secessionist forces have organized resistance, especially Port Harcourt and its regions etc. However, the return of the populations to normal life, and the end of war were simultaneously with that of development of equipment in terms of economic, social and urban development (see economic activities). This is at the local level, because the local government budgetary policy has no subsidies available to the municipals (but has their budgets) to conduct their own development projects (infra planning policy and housing). However, many who were poor became rich[1]. This explains the economic development of the delta population: transforming traditional habitations to modern and semi-habitats.

The intermediary role played by the authorities of the eastern Region before the creation of Rivers State between the development agencies and the development projects of the Federal Government are now handled by the delta people, especial rural development projects in the delta (this was the reason of the failure of the NDDB in its mission). However, economic revolution cause by the oil industry has promoted the emergence of social classes. The business classes, workers, the proletariats, businessmen, manufacturers and business tycoons. Indeed, the establishment of the Government in the Niger Delta has also created jobs in both private and public sectors. The citizens who were in exile returned to their home towns or to Port Harcourt in search of jobs. This movement of population

---

[1] The opposite is not negligible for a few of the rich also became poor, especially those who opposed or does not corporate with them (the secessionist authorities), but were doing fine before the civil war.

and housing modernization and self-development continue, although the authorities have no plans for them. This urban explosion and urbanization are observable at the tip of the nuclei of ancient delta towns and sites, hence the appearance of the "new layouts" for new neighbourhoods in the delta towns and cities.

Although, these areas are called new, there is no real planning as understood for new quarters. They are rather characterized by a group of houses round a courtyard. In addition, these neighbourhoods often lacks the accompanying facilities (drinking water, schools etc) and therefore most of these new quarters so created depend on the old neighbourhoods Except at Port Harcourt and some other towns where schools were integrated into these neighbourhoods.

9.2.0. The urban population

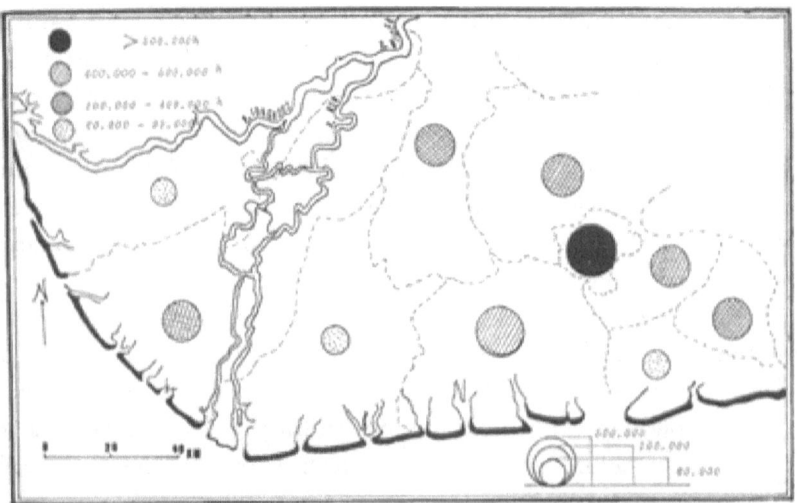

Fig 9.2: Urban growth in the 10 Local Government Authority Areas (2006)

Chapter 10

The urbanizing Activities

The main economic activities in the Niger Delta are fishing, transport (River) and trade. Although these three are the main activities carried out in the North, North-East, and North-West of the Delta where the land is drier. But agriculture does not count in the South, South-East and South-West. However, we are here interested in the evolution of the economic sector that has an influence on the development and urbanization (community, individual or collective) of the Niger Delta towns. The economy of the Niger Delta was flourishing at the time of the palm oil trade which was used for multiple purposes for the industry as a raw material and lubricant of mechanical equipment. The Niger Delta has been known for the production of this essential commodity. But now it is replaced by the crude oil (the black gold). The Niger Delta remains one of the largest producers of this crude oil to the global community. In fact, 80% of Nigerian oil is produced in the Niger Delta. The country's second port is located at Port Harcourt, making the Niger Delta a major provider of the national economy among the 36 States of the Country.

In the early twentieth century after the unification of the two major regions of Nigeria (North and South), the Niger Delta (East) forms part of the Eastern Region. So it was evident that the Eastern Region must have been the economically the richest Region, even before the unification. And in addition to the port of Port Harcourt which is the second port in the country to provide the necessary infrastructures for business and development of industrial infrastructure to the Region of Lagos. It was therefore not surprising that the Government of the Eastern Region was opposed to the creation of a State in the Coastal Niger Delta. However, this economic growth, push for development and trade have been limited or concentrated in the city of Port Harcourt[1] at the expense of other towns in the Delta for decades.

The country's industrial growth depends on the Niger Delta today. The first Nigerian refinery was built at Alesa-Eleme, near Port Harcourt. Unfortunately, due to political reasons, the modern refinery which was supposed to be constructed at where the raw materials are available is left out with an obsolete plant. Anyway, industrial infrastructures are largely concentrated around the cities of Port Harcourt, Warri, Sapele, Ughelli etc. The possibilities for expansion of these industries and installing new ones are unlimited (see industry). In the Delta as any other State in the country, the business activities are the responsibility of the Ministry of Trade and Industry. This Ministry consists of six main services: Administrative, Commerce, Cooperative, Inspection of Agricultural products, Industry and a service for Small and Medium Industries.

In fact, each of the Services is responsible for the matters concerning it: commerce for the promotion of trade, industry to make effective industrial policies in the region, cooperative register and supervising cooperatives societies and companies, inspection is responsible for determining quality of the agricultural products, while the service S.M.I and S.M.E[2] function to motivate the population to create industries and companies for the development and the establishment of new SMI and SME.

10.1.0. The petroleum Activities (fig 10.1)

After independence, the need for industrialization, the coastal Niger Delta and its people have played an important role, making Nigeria one of the largest oil producers. The first surveys were held in 1953 to the discovery of a natural gas field in Akata near Port Harcourt in January 1955. They began to find the first indications of oil and from 1956 to 1959, the discoveries multiplied[3] resulting in 1958 with a production of 300,000 t, which reached 370,000t in 1963. The deposits are located in the vicinity of Port Harcourt and the reserves were estimated at more than 130 million

---

[1]   Port Harcourt in the Eastern Delta and Warri, Sapele and Ughelli in the Western Delta.

[2]   S.M.I (Small and Medium Industries) and S.M.E (Small and medium Enterprises)

[3]   Geographic information: Crude Oil in Nigeria N° 5 November/December 1964 pp216-R 17.

tonnes. Three pipelines of 175 Km in total length evacuate the liquid to Port Harcourt from where it is shipped to Europe for refining. This motivated the construction of the first refinery in the Country at Alesa-Eleme near Port Harcourt. The outstanding Companies in the operations of the oil technology in the Niger Delta are Shell petroleum Development Company (Nig) Ltd; Agip, Elf, Texaco, Mobil and N.N.P.C[1].

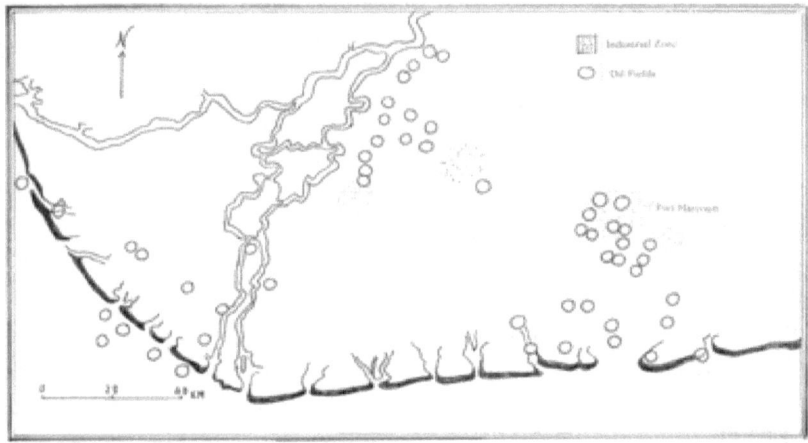

Fig 10.1: The distribution or locations of oil fields in the Eastern Niger Delta

Photo 10.1: An oil field at Oporoma.

---

[1]   Nigeria National Petroleum Company

One can notice the gas flame that burns day and night with the pumping plant on the left of the photo. Such burning flames are many in the Niger Delta. They are easily observable in the night.

10.2. The industrialization

Oil is not the only industrial activity in the Niger Delta, there are other viable businesses established in collaboration with the Government of the region (Rivers and Bayelsa States), foreign firms and indigenous enterprises. They are very numerous including: West African Glass Industries (Nig) Ltd; which produces bottles, the breweries which brews beers. The Nigerian Engineering Works (Nig) Ltd which produces air conditioners, refrigerator, fans, filling cabinets; the Eastern wrought Iron (Nig) ltd, which produces mattresses and high quality furniture; the Michelin (Nig) ltd, for tires, Metalloplastic for plastic items; and Machet Crocodile Company (Nig) ltd, manufacturer of knives, razors and other companies just to mention but few.

In addition to other manufacturing companies, such as Waterglass Boatyard at Marine base, Port Harcourt is manufacturers of speed boards and of high-speed vessels. All these activities create viable industrial jobs for all skilled workers, handlers, qualified employees.

Although, the country has major economic, industrial Companies in other parts, they are constantly making their appearances in the coastal Niger Delta. The Governments of the Niger Delta in 1988 has pursued a policy of rural industrialization by creating industrial zones in the 10 headquarters of the 10 Local Government Authority Areas. This is the opposite of the government's decision in 1987 to create only two small industries. However, two industrial zones have been created, one at Yenagoa and other at Ahoada for example. The Government's strategy is to continue to create these areas each year until each of the towns has its industrial zone.

In the Niger Delta, fishing is considered an occupation for all. They do it in one way or the other depending on the environment each is located. In fact, fish production in the Niger Delta was 194,479,000 T. in 1982; 166,567,000 T. (1983), 110,835,000 T. (1984), 67,383,000 T (1985) and 73,947,000 T. (1986). This makes the Niger Delta the largest producer of fish in the Country. In 1982, production counted for 39.11%, 33.19% (1983), 33.89% (1984), 33.46% (1985), 30.29% (1986) of the total production in the country. However, production of fish in the Delta does not cease to decline (since 1982). The Eastern part is more affected probably la population is turning towards other activities or water pollution from petroleum activities in the Delta.

10.2.1. Agriculture.

Although the Niger Delta lacks cultivable land, agriculture is practiced on an encouraging level (Photo 10.2). The fishing industry (including traditional fishing) which is part of the activities of the Delta people is among the sources of economic sectors that affect urbanization. People were living on fishing, construct, and educate their children and much more. The State Governments provide subsidies to farmers having land for cultivation to encourage agriculture and fish culture ponds.

Photo 10.2: The farm and the rice field at Peremabiri.

It is programmed to cover 2 500 h. The farm was established by the N. D. D. B. in 1964, one of the Government efforts to encourage the delta people to invest in agriculture.

10.2.2.0. Commercial Activities

The Niger Delta commercial unit is pretty good and the dynamic to its level compared to neighbouring States. Markets in rural areas and the development of local shops in urban areas: especially at the local government headquarters etc. A contradiction of the commercial mechanism is more sensitive in the wholesale trade services than in the retail sector. This has declined to 30.5% the number of the wholesale trade services on food[1].

The positive part (25%) of non-food whole trade services mainly to the significant development of commercial wood, tires, liquid gas and home furnishings.

At retail, it is rather an increase (48.2%) on the points of sale mainly from food shops, grocery and more specialized shops. These include fish markets, poultry, fruits and vegetables, while a significant decline (55%) comes from the bakery. This might probably due to the closing of the only plant of wheat flour at Port Harcourt which was supplying the whole eastern part of the country.

The progressive increase of the food sector to the non-food observed on the evolution of the number of business establishments by industry in 1980 to 1989 is a characteristic phenomenon of the delta since 1970. The towns in the delta had no big shopping centres except some cities like Port Harcourt, Warri etc, but today these centres and supermarkets are springing up like champignons in the delta towns. Although, from time immemorial all the delta towns and villages are having open public markets or open air and which are held on fixed days, weekly or daily.

The Delta cities/towns have developed generally privileged sites and somehow predestined to them to ensure the broad rear. For example Port Harcourt, Bonny, Akassa etc while none of them can no more expand beyond these favourable locations we called "urban site" Others may still hold some confluent basins, Bomadi, Sagbama or road, Yenagoa, Kaiama[2]. But others like Amassoma, Oporoma, Brass, Buguma, Degema etc owed their wealth to political or commercial activities. Sometimes both and much more than geographical or others through the existence of a Port: Port Harcourt, Bonny etc (fig 10.2). But the city of Port Harcourt exerts a

---

[1]   The results of our investigation on the evolution and closing time of commercial establishments at Port Harcourt (markets 2, Creek road, the market and night sales along the Ikwerre road mile2 in 1988 and 1989. It is difficult to determine precisely, because there are two groups of retailers, those in the day time and those in the evening (till night), however, the results is a representation of the objective of the study.

[2]   East-West Highway constructed in 1971 which passes through the town thereby dividing it into two.

regional, national and international[1] influence. Thanks to its Seaport and international Airport. During the pre-colonial period, the delta produced salt and dry fish. This trade continued until the arrival of the Europeans (Talbot 1932) especially the Portuguese and with the intervention of the slave trade, the delta became a commercial centre of attraction. This follows an introduction of new articles such as sea salt, dried fish from Norway, clothing, metal tools, glassware and firearms.

The abolition of the slave trade in 1807 had not brought to halt the importance and role of the region. Thus, abolition was followed by the trade in palm oil. However, the Niger Delta was recognized in 1889 on behalf of the Oil Rivers Protectorate in the conference of Berlin, a company, the "Royal Niger Company" was established in 1885. In 1893, British protectorate was extended further inside the territory and renamed the Protectorate of the Coastal Niger Delta (1896). When in 1900 after the revocation of the charter of the "Royal Niger Company" (2) the previous year, the territories of the Company came under the official control of the British Government.

The relative location of the Coastal Niger Delta from the Atlantic Ocean and the topographic conditions depending on the distance from the sea, that the delta provides ideal sites for the construction of ports. However, the delta provides the largest number of ports[2] of the Country (9 Ports). Their importance has enhanced the establishment of British Administration (British rule) that follows the construction of roads and railways that connect these ports to the interior, such as the ports of Port Harcourt, Warri, and Sapele have access to the Sea by road, due to the traffic intensity and scope they cover. Today, the coastal Niger Delta is the major producer of the Nigeria oil.

Port Harcourt, the Capital of Rivers State has an annual export of more than 1.36 million tons, the second in the Federation, its international airport and industrial zone that makes it the third largest industrial and commercial after Kano and Lagos in Nigeria. Its port and airport serving not only the Niger Delta, but also all the Eastern States of the Country, parts of the North and cargo transit to and from French Tchard.

---

[1]   The Port and Airport serves the Eastern States; the former Eastern Region of the country.

[2]   Established 1885.

Other ports such as Sapele harbour at the River Ethiope 928 km to the estuary (mouth) of the Escravos River (Fig 10.2)[1] which deserves the province of Benin-City, whose goods are predominantly wood and rubber from the inland of Sapele[2]. That of Abonnema is located at River Sombreiro and can be reached by Bonny River. Major commodities are palm kernels and palm oil from the East. Those of Warri and Burutu are said to be "Ocean-Niger harbours". The port of Warri is 40 km from the estuary of Forcados Town and has a series of short piers connected by floating bridges. This allows three ships to move in simultaneously. Most of these piers are owned by John Holt (Nig) Ltd. It also has a shipyard and a workshop. Burutu port is located on Island 8 km from the estuary of River Forcados. Burutu is also the terminus south of the River Transport Company of United African Company (U. A. C). The port of Bonny (Bonny terminal) principal activity is to load oil for export[3]. It is a harbour that overlooks the Atlantic Ocean, so easily accessible from the ocean.

The role of other harbours is rather tucked into themselves. That is, their influences and activities are almost limited to the Niger Delta and the nearby towns of the regional boundaries. Like any other regions or States of the Country, there are administrative centres.

---

[1]   Ports in the Country of which 9 are in the Coastal Niger Delta—Forcados, Burutu, Bonny, Brass, Bakana, Abonnema, Warri, Sapele, and Port Harcourt. Established in 1885.

[2]   The former home of the Oil River Protectorate.
There is a second harbour owned by a Sawmill and a plywood plant.

[3]   In the 17th century, the port of Bonny was used for the shipment of slaves bound for Europe.

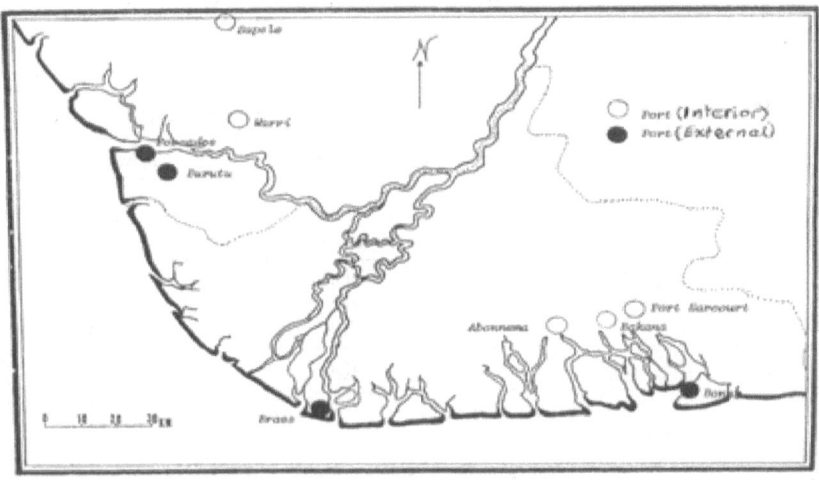

Fig 10.2: Towns in the Coastal Niger Delta Having Port (Harbour).

These headquarters does not necessarily mean that these towns are more populated or developed, but determined in some cases from its location or by political influence[1]. This is the case of Yenagoa, Oporoma, and Degema which are small towns in 1963, with populations of less than 5,000 inhabitants but where Headquarters or administrative districts while in the same year Buguma had a population of 14,609 inhabitants, and Amassoma had 11,185 inhabitants and are not.

The major role played by the Niger Delta yesterday and today is purely economic. We could say that Nigeria depends to some extent on the Niger Delta: Namely of raw materials oil (the black gold). Have there been any financial returns to the area?

10.2.3.0. Marine Activities

Without treating maritime policy of the Government, we would like to explain in a nutshell to quantify the areas that can specifically relate to maritime activities: The delta ports. This is the loading and unloading cargos in the international trade (Foreign Trade Cargo).

---

[1]   The influence of Politician of the town.

10.2.3.1. The Loading.

The total load in all the harbours in the delta was:

Year	Quantity National (tons)	Niger Delta %
1983	45,613,000	75.15
1984	52,841,000	84.98
1985	59,324,000	87.04
1986	56,795,000	86.14

Source: Nigerian Ports Authority

Table 10.1: Loading in the Delta Ports

In fact the majority of loading was recorded in the western delta. However, loading was 39.13% in 1983; 43.67% in 1984; 45.91% in 1985; 41.54 in 1986. While in the east of the delta loading was 36.02% in 1983; 41.34% in 1984; 41.13% in 1985; and 44.50% in 1986. There was a significant drop in quantity of cargo loaded in 1985 in the east (0.21%) and in the west for less then 4.27%. See also Appendices IV-A.

10.2.3.1. Unloading

The unloading cargos in the country had been declining steadily since 1983:

Year	Quantity National (tons)	Niger Delta (%)
1983	16,083,000	31.21
1984	11,633,000	26.02
1985	13,565,000	23.16
1986	9,850,000	21.14

Table 10.2: Unloading in the delta ports

In fact, contrary to the figures of the loading, most of the unloading (Appendices IV-B) was made in the eastern Delta. However, the unloading was 18.19% in 1983; 14.05% in 1984; 12.79% in 1985; 14.02% in 1986. This is due probably to a change in policy by the Federal Government on importation.

10.2.3.2. The distillation of alcohol

A distillation of alcohol is for some towns and villages in the Niger Delta their first food industry. For example, in the towns along the Rivers Forcados and Nun (freshwater area), the alcohol production was considered a profession that generates an income. It has been so since centuries, but it (alcohol) was considered an illegal product while the whisky was legal. This contradicting opinion gave rise to debates that led to the legalization of the alcohol "Ogogoro" produced from the local industries in 1967. Before this time, it was sold illegally. Today, it has become a source of income and is sold publicly everywhere in the country. Its production is declining in the delta these days due to ameliorations of conditions of life and the creation of states.

The raw material for its production is the palm wine especially from the raphia palm. The distiller in some cases settles in the forest for some days to distil it. The raphia palm tree is spread over swampy areas, but the distiller looks for an area where they are in abundance. This enables him to get the palm wine which is the raw material for its production without going long distances from the camps where his distillation is implanted. The process, principle of distillation and the plant layout seems to be scientific, but the materials or facilities (equipment) are purely artisanal (home made). Alcohol is much sought in the delta society in all ceremonies and receptions especially traditional meetings, therefore, its importance among the Delta people and their societies.

The quantity of production is large enough or to make more profit, that they supply other towns such as Lokoja, Onitsha, Lagos, Warri and even to Tiko and Duala local markets in Cameroon. It should be noted that the sale by dealers and distillers always skips audit authorities, but only within Nigeria, is tax free like any other local sectors. Unfortunately, this lucrative profession is fading away or declining to extinction.

Chapter 11

Housing and Accommodation

11.1. The issue of housing.

The issues of urban housing in the Coastal Niger Delta have increased more in recent years. Port Harcourt seems the only city where people believe in the delta to find a better social life. The decentralization policy has not given a significant diminution to migration from other cities to Port Harcourt. As a result, the population of Port Harcourt continues to grow and thus the gap between the number of housing demand and housing provided increases more and more. In another issue is the rapid growth of population since the post civil war, due to the returning citizens of the State living in other States during the war and rural-urban migration[1]. The creation of the Local Government Authority Areas does not solve the problem though there was a slight diminution, but increase the problem in these local Government Authority Areas.

Rivers State was divided into two States, making Rivers and Bayelsa States on the 1st October, 1996 with Yenagoa as the Capital of the State. The creation of Bayelsa State shows a brutal increase in the vacant rooms at Port Harcourt, though some of the Bayelsans still maintained their rooms and apartments. Yenagoa, itself was not prepared to receive such a population coupled with again the rural-Urban migration. Yenagoa being the Capital had a greater scarcity of accommodation than as experienced

---

[1]   Port Harcourt is the only major city in the Eastern delta and also the only city to have both an International airport and an international seaport in the Eastern part of the country.

at Port Harcourt. Port Harcourt was in some way prepared to receive incoming population as regards equipment compared to Yenagoa.

The Bayelsa State Government, to solve the scarcity of accommodation embanked on housing programmes for the Commissioners and other low cost housing estates which are all in progress. The programme is followed up fortunately by the successful administrations since when it was launched. Amassoma also had a brutal increase in her population when the Niger Delta University was opened in 2000 with an initial population of over 2000 persons were added to the population of Amassoma (38 790 h). In the 2001/2002 academic session the added population raised to over 13,000. This was not prepared for, though the University provided accommodation, which are themselves over populated, there are also none residential students and members of staff. Thus the need for the Government to extend the housing programmes to meet up such brutal needs. Until today, it is the combined efforts of the indigenes to meet up the needs for accommodation. This is just one example of crucial shortage of housing in the towns of the Coastal Niger Delta.

11.2.0. Land Ownership

One of the most significant forces of growth known only by the Niger Delta resides in the importance of the changes affecting land use in some areas:

(a). Concentration of population in the towns/villages and the labour force expansion of the urban area in particular Port Harcourt and a radius of at least eight kilometres on the western axis: Including other towns/cities of the headquarters of the Local Government Authority Areas.
(b). Transformation of rural areas due to rural exodus as well as the decentralization of public services, rural industrialization and so on.

The importance of this transformation of land use has become so since 1970. However, it is necessary that public authorities involved actively ensuring control of the ground. This determines the performance of any planning policy. As a result, the Federal Government in 1978 passed a decree giving the country all land and the underground to the Federal Government.

The Niger Delta lands are communal or family origin. However, in some rural areas, land or plot to construct a house was usually free. It has changed since the houses have become an investment and not only for family living homes. Indeed, customary law gives jurisdiction to the tribal chiefs and heads of families to control the use and destination of the land. As a result, the planning of each town depends on the head of the community. This has caused the lack of planning of towns and villages in the Niger Delta. This is where the towns in the Niger Delta need not only the community, but also the assistance of Governments Agents.

The ordinance of 1917 relating to the acquisition of land for public use concerned only the acquisition of land required. However, land belongs to either a family or a community. But under the 1978 decree and the ordinance of 1917, the Government or Public Authorities or individuals may acquire the land required for public (Government) project by expropriation. In fact, public Authorities are only able to carry out public facilities, which imply that they possess or acquire the necessary land only by expropriation. The land issue is a must, it has been raised for a long time and the planning law gives the public[1] a number of steps as it will be necessary to determine, if they are adequate and effective.

---

[1]   The public Authority: the Federal Government, the Regional Government and the Local Authorities.

Chapter 12

The urban network

The relational systems in the urban network of the Niger Delta can be classified into two categories: (a) the modern system by administrative means and economic activities (b) the traditional system.

Rivers State		Rivers State	Bayelsa State
A (Before 1984)	**B** (1984-1995)	**A** (1996)	**C** (2010)
State Capital Port Harcourt	State Capital Port-Harcourt	State Capital Port-Harcourt	State Capital Yenagoa
L. G. A. Hq. Ex. Degema	L. G. A. Hq. Ex Yenagoa	L. G. A. Hq. Ex Ahoada	L.G.A. Hq. Ex Sagbama
Urban Council Ex. Amassoma	District Council Ex Oporoma	District Council	Urban Council Ex Amassoma
Community Council Ex Amatolo	Electoral section Ex Alomu II (ward 20)		

Table 12.1: The Urban Hierarchies.

The difficulty in capturing urban networks[1] in the Niger Delta since 1967 is that every change of administration is often followed by a reorganization of the existing networks. However, we are considering

---

[1]   The system of relations in the urban network.

from 1984 to 1996 there are already three. The first since the creation of Rivers State in 1967 and 2010 (Bayelsa State) are both hierarchies above.

In fact, the organization is generally at the State level and based primarily on existing public facilities in the town. Such towns are not necessarily large cities by size or by population, but by the presence of some equipment and structures of public service. For instance Oporoma, Degema, Brass, etc while others by the presence of a road connected to the Capitals Yenagoa and other towns other towns: Sagbama, Kaiama, etc.

Apart from the colonial hierarchy that the Authorities continue to reorganize until today, the reality is at any other level, especially in the Niger Delta province. We can identify two areas of influence that contain three major cities, area in the Western part of the Delta which hosts the towns of Warri and Sapele, while the other area is the home to the City of Port Harcourt (fig 12.1). These cities are home to branches of banks, homes, businesses, subsidiaries of large industrial companies, agents of the rule of industrial powers. They are also the seat of political power and place of residence of the rich fraction of the society, so that these towns become the locations of substitution industries and the attractions for rural people and other neighbouring regions of the country.

These three cities are cities with harbour (Port), particularly Port Harcourt, in addition has an international Airport that serves the major part of the Eastern[1] part of the country. It thus provides a fundamental link with the developed countries based on the export of raw materials[2] and the import of manufactured goods (products).

There are a number of towns mainly devoted to commercial activities (fig 12.1). They have now become in some way, centres of influence. These towns and villages are generally ordinary towns and villages, without any administrative importance.

---

[1]   States of Imo, Rivers, Ananbra and some of the Northern States.

[2]   Including petroleum.

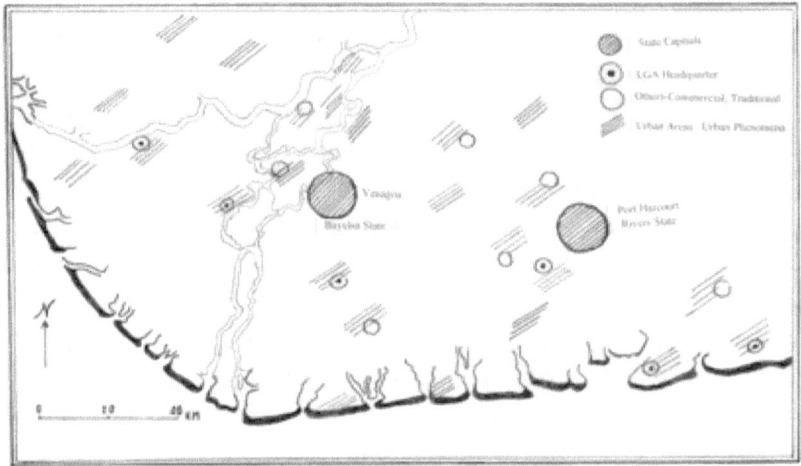

Fig 12.1: The urban phenomena and administratively classified urban towns.

However, the Niger Delta society has a complex and a more diverse urban hierarchy that some aspects recalling urban systems of the developed countries including Britain. In fact, it should be noted that all these small and medium towns, that surround, hold poorly demographic growth brutally. As a result, the population ratio of excess rural areas accumulated mainly in the cities, Port Harcourt, Warri, and Sapele. There follows a loss of equilibrium between economic growth and population growth. This has resulted in the lack of housing for the population surplus, the spontaneous proliferation of habitat and increased crime rate and divaricating crime.

The coastal Niger Delta is formed by a multiplicity of clans. The towns that make up each clan themselves as a family, which is within each clan, there is a traditional capital[1] which is the centre of influence where the Ebenanaowei (the clan head) resides. For example: Boma clan, town of influence, Ekowe; Ogboin clan, town of influence, Amassoma; Kalabari clan, town of influence is Buguma while Degema is the Local Government administrative capital. These and other traditional relationships make the Niger Delta one of the provinces that have a system of complex relationships. In fact, the complexity of these systems (traditional relationships) in addition to the relation of political and

---

[1]   The Capital has nothing to do with government administrative systems in the province.

administrative factors often results in a transformation of the system[1]. Indeed the establishment of new relational system city/town is brutal and contemporary evolution characterized by the formation or the creation of a market or a particular portion of highway example Kaiama and Patani[2]. The evolution of the conditions of a town in the Niger Delta is control in general by the modifications of the system. That is, the flexible use of means of transport and business services. In this way, the town and villages are actually involved in the geographical hierarchy. The momentum in the urban system comes from industry and local or domestic demand provides the main opportunity. There are villages that do not play a secondary role. The rural consumption will further reduce consumption by urban growth. While rural production (goods) loses its value on each day compared to urban production and services.

In addition, this self-determination of these towns also affirmed by the population growth. The economic development, agricultural and the rural society emphasize the bursting of relationships between town/village and within: for example the residents of Amassoma and its neighbours. Trade practices such as occurring in the system of relationships between town/village/city.

However, the level of development of these network systems are distinguished from each other in size, population or tertiary facilities in the towns that make up each of these networks. Cities like Port Harcourt, Warri, Sapele, each have three characteristics. Unfortunately, they better meet the needs of the inhabitants of these cities as a real power of organization of environment. It seemed that the system of relations the inhabitants of these cities as a real power of organization of environment. It seemed that the system of relations in these cities remains the fractions of the populations who have access to the use of services and facilities.

In fact the petroleum production does not provide a deltaic town/ city an animation function of the provincial economy. However, towns are limited to their roles as a drainage of raw fish . . . of the Province; the animation function is performed through the system in operation is the organization of the local transport etc.

---

[1]   Of the rural system in the urban system.

[2]   The town of Kaiama is traversed by the highway of "East-West by pass" while the town of Patani is connected by a direct road to Lagos, and has a market.

In the Eastern Niger Delta, urban organization is based on the city of Port Harcourt. However, Port Harcourt, a port city which is the second largest port in the country concentrates most of the tertiary of the country that organizes the export of petroleum products[1] and the import of manufactured goods necessary to the three Eastern States[2] of the country.

12.1.0. Urban conditions

The general urban conditions in the Coastal Niger Delta are the conditions that we encounter during our research. These are elements of the problems of the Delta.

By universal definition, the most important trend of urbanization and urban dynamics is based on modern industrial technology. In addition, highly concentrated to be selective, we can predict the emergence of a few cities in the prospects of development and urbanization in the Coastal Niger Delta. We can conjecture four development zones across the delta around Port Harcourt (eastern delta), Warri, Sapele, and Ughelli (western delta).

In fact, such a concentration aggravates rather than solves the problems of balanced development for the entire region. It is therefore clear that the Coastal Niger Delta needs a policy of urbanization that must be formulated and based on the region. This policy must be integrated into a wider context of the definition for economic development and spatial planning of the Delta region.

However, for the towns in the delta region to play effectively the role of a pole of development in its economy as a major provider of the Country's economy calls for a review by the administration (Federal Government), State governments and of the administrative divisions of the Niger Delta. This requires the possibility for the Authorities to provide the means to generate income and to define a policy for collecting statistical data for development and urban expansion. Most important, to ensure that contracts on projects awarded be carried to its term or be completed, for it was observed that most of the contracts awarded to contractor were abandoned on the way, while the Government seems to have paid completely (fully). This is one of the anti-development factors in the region. The success of these strategies of the Government in the

---

[1]   And Bonny Terminal.

[2]   Rivers State, Anambra State and Imo State.

Delta requires it's efficiency and the power of completing their projects of development and planning that must take into account the peculiarities of towns and areas in general[1]. Is a question of management and organization for urban dynamics in the Niger Delta? And the Authorities do not take any legal means to see that these Contractors complete their jobs. A job half done is work not done.

We have in our research could identify the constraints linked to the expansion of the towns in the Coastal Niger Delta. These are the geographical constraints and are part of the problems of erosion, flooding and flood, while the human constraints are related to the management and organisation within the various Authorities in the region and the State Governments. It is from these geographical and human constraints observed that we are committed to provide techno-economic solutions compatible with the natural environment and human through a part of an overall development, the Government and axis to administrative organization of the region.

In fact, throughout the course of our research, we encountered three main problems: flooding, erosion and topography linked to natural and artificial ponds. Our proposals for an overall development[2] or partial[3] against these natural phenomena take into account the reality of the natural and human environment, as we have observed in our field studies and on our models. It falls perhaps not into any existing theory or principle. The transposition of western models, management and techniques may not be applicable to the natural and urban environment of the Niger Delta region. These techniques have been studied and applicable to the environment in which they are intended, because the changes in climatic, environmental or topographic conditions can effectively changes the result of an effective technique to failure.

Finally, our proposals are designed specifically to fight against natural constraints on the extension[4] of towns in the Niger Delta by taking into account however, the economic and financial conditions in the region. However, we propose a technique compatible with all major constraints.

The recommendations and techniques will not be included in this volume as it contained case studies and detailed intensive research of some selected towns in each of the areas defined in this volume.

---

[1] Fresh or brackish water areas.

[2] At the regional level.

[3] At the local level and municipal level

[4] As the living environment of urban residents of the Niger Delta.

APPENDICES

Appendix I

Administrative evolution of Nigeria from the colonial era.

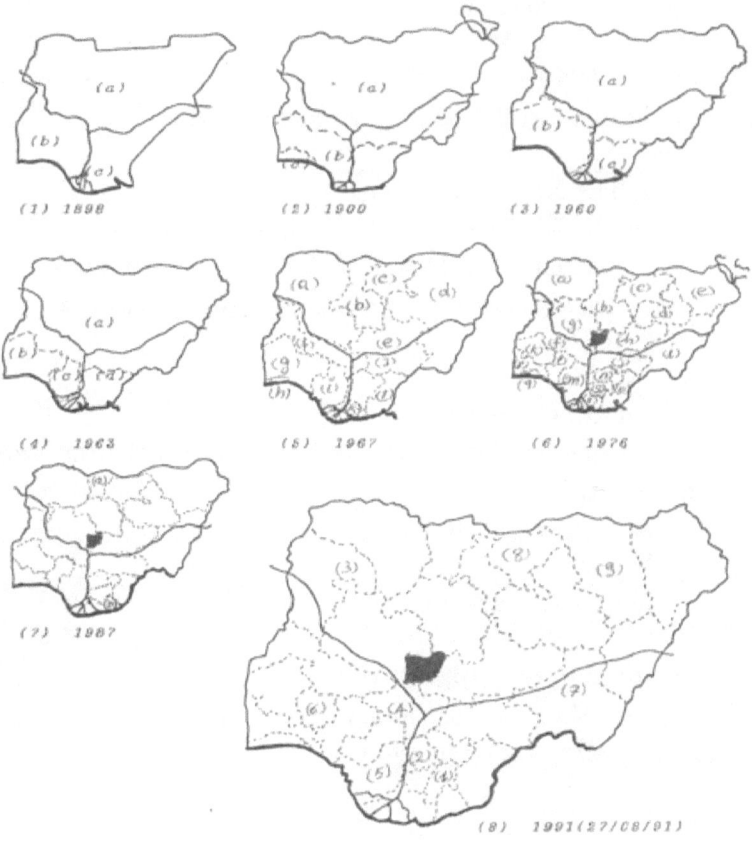

(1) 1898   (2) 1900   (3) 1960

(4) 1963   (5) 1967   (6) 1976

(7) 1987

(8) 1991(27/08/91)

The evolution of states in Nigeria since the colonial period (see maps above):

(1) The situation in 1898

There were three areas of administrative authorities.

(a) The area under the authority of the Royal Niger Company.

(b) The Lagos protectorate

(c) The Niger Coast Protectorate

(2) The situation in 1900

The situation of the three protectorates that lasted from 1900 to 1914 (they were united for the birth of Nigeria in 1914).

(a) The North Protectorate

(b) The Protectorate of Southern

(c) The protectorate of Lagos

(3) Status in 1960

The division into three regions after independence on October 1, 1960

(a) The Northern Region.

(b) The Western Region (including the portion of the western coastal Niger Delta).

(c) The Eastern Region (including the eastern coastal Niger Delta)

(1) The situation in 1963

The division into four regions at the end of the status of Republic in 1963

(a) Northern Region

(b) Western Region

(c) Eastern Region including Delta (East)

(5) The situation in 1967

The division of the country in 12 states at the end of the First Republic after a coup in 1966

(a) North West State

(b) North Central State

(c) Kano State

(d) North-East State

(e) Benue-Plateau State

(f) Kwara State

(g) Western State

(h) Lagos State

(i) Mid-west State (including the western part of the delta

(j) East-central State

(k) Rivers State (Eastern delta)

(l) South-East State

(2) The situation in 1976

The division into 19 states and change of names of states bearing names of the cardinal points as:

(a) Sokoto State

(b) Kaduna State

(c) Kano State

(d) Bauchi State

(e) Borno State

(f) Kwara State

(g) Niger State

(h) Plateau State

(i) Gongola State

(j) Benue State

(k) Oyo State

(l) Ondo State

(m) Bendel State including the western part of the Niger delta.

(n) Anambra State

(o) Cross-River State

(p) Ogun State

(q) Lagos State

(r) Rivers State (the eastern Niger Delta)

(s) Imo State

The Federal Capital Territory

(7) The situation in 1987

Two new states were created in 1976 by the situation in all 21 states

(a) Katsina State

(b) Akwa Ebom State

(8) The situation in 1991 (August 27)

Division into 30 states to prepare the country for political stability and social integration in 1992 to civilian rule.

The new states created in addition to the states in the situation of 1987 are:

N°	State	**Capital**
1	Abia	Umuahia
2	Anambra	Awka
3	Kebbi	Birmin Kebbi
4	Kogi	Locoja
5	Delta	Asaba
6	Osun	Oshogbo
7	Taraba	Jalongo
8	Jigawa	Dutse
9	Yobe	Damaturu

Thus were also created 47 new local government authorities and authorities of each of the Local Government (new and old) is a Federal District

(9) The situation in 1996

Six more States were created in this year, making a total of 36 States in the country till today 2011.

They are:
(1) Bayelsa State
(2) Ebonyi State
(3) Ekiti State
(4) Gombe State
(5) Nassarawa State
(6) Zamfara State

B-The classification of Nigerian towns/cities in 1919

1ˢᵗ Category: Lagos

	Southern Provinces	Northern Provinces
2ⁿᵈ Category are :	Aba	Ilorin
	Abiokuta	Kaduna
	Calabar	Kano
	Enugu Ngwo	Lokoja
	Itu	Minna
In the Niger Delta:	Onitsha	Zaria
	Opoko	
	Ibadan	

3ʳᵈ Category:	Forcados
	Port Harcourt
	Sapele
	Warri

Southern Provinces

Aba*	Asaba	Ikom	Obudu	Uyo
Abak	Awka	Ikorodu	Ogoja	Uzuakoli
Abakaliki	Badagri	Ikot-Ikpene	Ogwashi	

In the Delta

Ado	Benin	Ilaro	Okigwi	Ahoada
Afikpo	Eket	Koko	Omohia	Bonny
Agbo	Epe	Kwale	Ondo	Brass
Arochuku	Ife	Obubra	Oron	Burutu
Arochuku	Ijebu-Ode	Owerri	Ubiaja	Degema

*Aba was downgraded from 2ⁿᵈ Category due to lost of its commercial function etc.

<u>Northern Provinces</u>

Abiusi	Bauchi	Jebba	Offa
Ankpa	Bida	Kontagora	Sokoto
Baro	Ibi	Maiduguri	Zungeru

Source: Nigeria Handbook 1919

An observation of this list reveals that the definition appears appropriate in most of the cities especially in the East where they numbered twenty-two, while not appropriate for cities such as Ife, Ijebu-Ode, Benin and Sokoto. Because these cities had a large population centre and were ancient cities

Appendix II

1. The 5 Districts and the 17 County Councils in the Eastern Delta (Rivers State)

(1) Ahoada Division

- Abua County Council

- Ekpeye Engenni County Council

- Etche County Council

- Ikwerre County Council

- Obio Urban County Council

- Ogba/Egbema County Council

(2) Brass Division

- Nembe County Council
- Ogbia County Council
- Southern Ijaw County Council
- Northerm Ijaw County Council

(3) Degema Division

- Kalabari County Council
- Bonny County Council
- Okrika County Council

(4) Ogoni Division

- Khana County Council
- Gokana County Council
- Eleme County Council

(5) Port Harcourt Division

- Port Harcourt Municipal Council

2. The new Administrative Divisions created in 1989 (Eastern Delta)

(1) Ahoada Local Gouvernment Area

(2) Brass   "   "   "

(3) Bonny   "   "   "

(4) Port Harcourt   "   "

(5) Degema   "   "   "

(6) Asaritoru   "   "   "

(7) Obio/Akpor   "   "

(8) Okrika   "   "   "

(9) Etche   "   "   "

(10) Ikwerre   "   "   "

(11) Khana-Oyigbo   "   "

(12) Go-Khana-Tai Eleme   "

(13) Yenagoa   "   "   "

(14) Sagbema   "   "   "

Appendix III

A. The mission of the Niger Delta Basin Development Authority (N.D.B.D.A)

(1) To undertate comprehensive development of both surface and underground water resources for multi-purpose use

(2) To undertate schemes for the control of floods and afforestation

(3) To construct and maintain dams, dykes, poldens, wells, borcholes, irrigation and drainage systemes and other works necessaty for the achievement of the Authority's fonctions under this section

(4) To provide water from reservoirs and lakes under the control ef the Authority for irrigation purposes to farmers and re conised associations as well as for urbain water supply schemes for a fee to be determined by the Authority concerned, with the approval by the Ministry

(5) The control of pollution in Rivers, lakes, lagoons and creeks in the Authority's area in accordance with nationally laid dawn standards.

(6) To ressettle persons affected by the works and schmes specified in this section or under spécial resettement schemes

(7) To develop fisheries and improve navigation on the rivers, lakes, reservoirs, lagoons and creeks in the Authoriry's area

(8) To indertake the mechanited clearing and cultivation of land for the production of crops and livestock and for forestry in areas both inside irrigation projets for a fee to be determined by the Authority concerned with the approval of the Ministry

(9) To underface the large-scale multiplication of improved seeds, livestock and tree scedlings for distribution to farmers and for afforestation schems

(10) To process crops, livestock products by farmers in the Authority's area in partnership with State agencies and amy other person

(11) To assist the state and local Gouverment in the implementation of the following rurakl development work in the Authority's area

(12) The construction of small dams, wells and borehodes and development of waterways for the evacuation of farm product

(13) The provision of power for oural electrfication schemes from suitable irrigation dams and other types of power stations under the control of the Authority concerned

(14) The establishment of agro-service centres

(15) The establishment of grazing reserves end

(16) The training of staff for the running and maintenance of rural development schemes and for general extension work at the village level

B. The projects completed by the N.D.B.D.A

(1) Preremabiri Rice project

(2) Community Fish farm development

(3) Sagbema River project (Forcados)

(4) Isampou River project (Nun)

(5) Erosion ad flood control

(6) Rural water supply

(7) Yenagoa oil palm Estate

(8) Andoni river projecct :

    . Large scale vegetale scheme

    . Artisanal Fisheries Development

    . Trawl Fisheries Development

(9) Nun river project

    . Village rice scheme

    . Raphia palm project

    . Jetty construction

    . Land reclamation and water improvement

    . Head quarters development

(10) Orashi River poject

    . Integrated piggery project

    . Integrated poultry project

    . Mangrove Products industrial complex

    . Scholl of vocational agriculture

    . integrated cassava and garri production scheme cattle ranch

C. The functions of the community development Committee (CDC)

There are 11 functions; its mission is to play an advisory role in the joint operation of the development of the towns. Its functions are:

1. Planning and execution of projects of common
2. Communications Agent (information)
3. Support activities of DPRRI RAIRDEP
4. Agent for the collection of public revenue
5. An intermediary to negotiate for payment of Subventions for town projects.
6. To promote continued education levels in the public schools.
7. Agent of planning and development
8. Protection of public facilities
9. Agent of environmental protection and health
10. Agent for the maintenance of law and order
11. To assist local authorities in the recovery of income

Appendix IV

A. Foreign Trade Cargo Loaded

PORTS	1983	1984	1985	1986
Apapa (Lagos)	230	88	178	221
Fed. Lighter Terminal	8	4	23	15
Calabar	44	17	75	60
Qua-Iboe (Eket)	14 759	9 209	8 539	8 785
Tincan Island	45	25	15	55
Port Harcourt	35	43	31	78
Okrika	343		940	972
Bonny	15 255	18 670	19 192	21 403
Brass	6 230	6 737	7 292	6 719
Warri	89	37	1 113	852
Sapele	11	7		
Escravos	4 091	4 259	6 691	7 884
Forcados	17 423	19 669	21 292	15 740
Pennington	2 134	3 168	2 199	2 977
Merryland (Bonny)		258	574	170
E - Delta	21 865	25 708	28 029	29 340
	36,02 %	41,34 %	41,13 %	44,50 %
W - Delta	23 748	27 139	31 235	27 453
	39,13 %	43,64 %	45,91 %	41,64 %
E + W Delta Total	45 613	52 841	59 324	56 795
	75,15%	84,98 %	87,04 %	86,14 %
Total Country	60 699	62 184	68 154	65 931

Ports in the Delta

Source: Nigeria Ports Authority

B-Foreign Trade Cargo Unloaded

PORTS	1983	1984	1985	1986
Apapa (Lagos)	8 489	6 432	6 720	5 211
Fed. Lighter Terminal	259	139	148	105
Calabar	149	126	339	179
Tincan Island	2 161	1 908	2 608	2 076
Port Harcourt	2 947	2 426	/	/
Okrika	500	355	381	635
Warri	1 115	714	976	495
Koko	89	21	56	20
Sapele	257	206	377	186
Escravos	633	452	/	/
Merryland (Bonny)	/	/	608	197
E - Delta	2 926	1 634	1 733	1 381
	18,19 %	14,05 %	12,78 %	14,02 %
W - Delta	2 094	1 393	1 409	701
	13,02 %	11,97 %	10,39 %	7,12 %
Total Delta	5 020	3 027	3 142	2 082
	31,21 %	26,02 %	23,16 %	21,14 %
Total Country	16 083	11 633	13 565	9 850

Source: Nigerian Ports Authority

Appendix V

LG A	A km²	1963		1986		1987		1988	
		Pop	D km²	Pop	D km²	Pop	D km²	Pop	D km²
1	AHOADA	2 490	179 339	72,03	318 709	128,00	329 602	132,37	335 035	134,55
2	BONNY	992	128 749	129,79	228 806	1 330,65	234 606	236,50	240 529	242,47
3	BORI	859	170 509	198,49	303 002	352,74	310 676	361,57	318 530	370,81
4	BRASS	2 760	126 206	45,73	224 285	81,26	229 968	83,32	235 774	85,43
5	DEGEMA	2 530	277 064	109,51	492 377	194,62	504 839	199,54	517 611	204,59
6	IKWERRE/ETCHE	2 380	201 849	84,81	358 511	150,72	367 793	154,54	377 094	158,44
7	OKRIKA/OYIGBO/TAI/ELEME	609	163 629	268,68	290 783	477,48	298 147	489,57	305 695	508,96
8	PORT HARCOURT	360	234 672	651,87	659 521	1 832,00	690 599	1 918,33	723 208	2 008,91
9	SAGBAMA	2 540	104 253	41,04	185 269	72,94	189 964	74,79	194 767	76,68
10	YENAGOA	3 900	180 770	46,60	323 031	82,83	331 210	84,93	339 587	87,07
		19 420	1 768 032	914,04	3 384 494	174,28	3 487 405	179,58	3 590 726	184,90

Source (1) Ministry of Housing and Environment, Port Harcourt Rivers State

Pop = Population; Den = Density; A = Area; L.G.A = Local Government Area

L G A = Local Government Area; A = Area; Pop = Population; Den = Density.

A. The total population and densities of the 10 Local Government Areas since 1963 (East Delta).

		11963	11983	Gt	%	11983	11990	Gt	%
1	AHOADA	179 339	298 233	118 894	66,30	298 233	351 996	53 763	15,27
2	BONNY	128 749	212 424	83 675	64,99	212 424	252 706	40 282	15,94
3	BORI	170 509	281 102	110 601	64,87	281 102	334 656	53 554	16,00
4	BRASS	126 206	208 072	81 866	64,87	208 072	247 710	39 638	16,00
5	DEGEMA	277 064	456 796	179 732	64,87	456 796	543 815	87 019	16,00
6	IKWERRE/ETCHE	201 849	332 790	130 941	64,87	332 790	396 184	63 394	16,00
7	OKRIKA/OYIGBO/TAI/ELEME	163 629	269 776	106 147	64,87	269 776	321 171	51 395	16,00
8	PORT HARCOURT	234 672	574 695	340 023	144,88	574 695	797 337	222 642	27,92
9	SAGBAMA	104 253	171 880	67 627	64,87	171 880	204 627	32 747	16,00
10	YENAGOA	180 770	299 502	117 812	64,81	295 582	356 779	61 197	17,15
		1 768 032	3 105 350	1 337 318	75,64	3 105 350	3 772 507	667 157	17,68

Source: Population of Nigeria 1963, Eastern Region Vol. I
and Vol. II (Western Region)

Gt = Growth

B. The evolution of the total Population in the 10 LGAs since 1963 (The Eastern Delta)

Appendix VI

The Ijaw native Authority established by the native Authority ordinance of 1943

A-The Eastern Delta Ijaws

Calabar	Opobo	Opobo Town		Opobo Town Council	Opobo Town
		Andoni		Andori Oru	Andoni Tribal
Rivers	Brass	Easter Ijaw central	Easter Ijaw central	Easter Ijaw central cuncil	Eastern Ijaw Sub Tribal
		Akassa		Akassa Clan Council	Akassa clan
		Apoi		Apoi clan cuncil	Apoi Clan
		Bassan		Bassan clan cuncil	Bassan clan
		Bomo		Bomo Clan cuncil	Bomo Clan
		Ekpetiama		Ekpetiama Clan cuncil	Ekpetiama clan
		Gbaran		Gbaran Clan cuncil	Gbaran Clan
		Ogboin		Ogboin Clan cuncil	Ogboin Clan
		Okodia Busseni		Okodia Busseni	Okodia Busseni
		Zarama		Zarama Group Council	Zarama Group
		Opokuma		Opokuma Clan Council	Opokuma Clan
		Oporoma		Oporoma Clan Council	Oporoma Clan
		Trakiri		Trakiri Clan Council	Trakiri Clan
		Tungbo		Tungbo Clan Council	Tungbo Clan
		Epir-Atissa		Epir-Atissa Group	Epir-Atissa Group
		Nembe		Nembe Clan Council	Nembe Clan
		Ogbeyan		Ogbeyan Clan Council	Ogbeyan Clan

A. The western Delta Ijaw

Rivers (suite)	Brass (suite)	Ayama	Ogbeyan	Ayama group council	Ayam group
		Emeya	"	Emeya group council	Emeya Group
		Oloibiri	"	Oloibiri Group Council	Oloibiri Group
	Degema	Bonny		Bonny Clan Council	Benni clan Area
		Kalabari		Kalabari clan council	Kalabari Clan
		Odual (Saka)		Odual (Saka)	Odual (Saka) clan
		Okrika		Okrika clan	Okrika Clan

Ondo	Okitipupa	Ijaw-Apoi district		Ijaw Apoi clan Council	Ijaw-Apoi district
		OndoArigba Dist		The Agadagba of Arigbod cuncil	Arcgbo district
Warri	Western Ijaw	Wester Ijaw central		Wester Ijaw central executive cuncil	western Ijaw Div.
		Benni clan Area	Wester Ijaw central	Benni Clan Council	Benni clan Area
		Iduwini Clan Area		Iduwi clan cuncil	Iduwini Clan Area
		Oporoza clan area		Oporoza clan cuncil	Oporoza clan
		Mein Clan area		Mein Clan cuncil	Mein Clan
		Ogula Clan area		Ogula Clan cuncil	Ogula Clan area
		Oporemor Clan area	Western Ijaw	Oporemor Clan cuncil	Oporemor Clan
		Seimbri Clan area		Seimbri Clan cuncil	Seimbri Clan
		Tarakiri Clan area		Tarakiri Clan cuncil	Tarakiri Clan area
		Tuomo Clan area		Tuomo Clan cuncil	Tuomo Clan

BIBLIOGRAPHY

General History Reference Books on Nigeria:

1. AFIGBO (A.E): Oral tradition and history of Eastern Nigeria (an essay in historical methodology of Africa) Notes III 3 April 1966. Pp 12-20, Ibid IV and 1er Oct. 1966 pp 17-27.
2. AYANDELE (E.A): The missionary impact on Nigeria 1842-1914: A political and social analysis Longmans 1966.
3. BUHLER (Jean): Tuez-les tous, guerre de sécession au Biafra. Photos de l'auteur-Paris Flammarion 1968 in 8° 237 pl. 5.
4. CROWDER (Michael): The story of Nigeria, London Faber and Faber 1962 in 8-307 pp pl. 1 t carts bibliog. Index.
5. GBAYEGA (Alex): Local Government reforms in Nigeria, ed. Willey & Sons 1983 pp 225-247—Carts table. 24 cm.
6. ISICHEI (E): A history of Nigeria, Longmans 1983 pp10-11.
7. KINSLEY (M): West African Studies London Macmillan 1899 pp. 443-566.
8. RENARD (Alain): Biafra naissance d'une nation Paris Aubier-Montaigne 1969 18 cm 255p Cartes
9. ADEJUWON (J.O) : Soil and the anthropos derivatives of the tropical rain forest in Nigeria (Nig) geogr 1973
10. ADENIYI (E.O): The impact of the change in river regime on economic activities below the Kanji dam Nigeria 1970
11. AJAGBO (H): Urban and rural development in Nigeria London, Heinemann 1976
12. BALTIMORE, HOPKINS (J): The economic development of Nigeria 1960 606p Carts, table-intern Bank for construction and development, Nigeria
13. BUCHANA (K.M) & PUCH (J.C): Land and people in Nigeria. The human geography of Nigeria and its environmental

background, London University Press ltd 1955 in 8° XII 257p. Fig pl. carts appendix.

14. Central office of information: Le Nigéria: Naissance d'une nation, London 1960 70p. cartes tabla. Graph.

15. EKANEM (I) : The 1963 Nigeria census: A critical appraisal Benin, Ethiope 1972

16. FLOYD (B): Eastern Nigeria: A geographical review, New York 1969 359p carts.

17. HELLEINER (Gerald K): Typology in development theory. The Lands surplus economy of Nigeria: Food research Inst. Of Studies Vol. VI n° 2 1966 pp 181-194

18. IGBOZURIKE (Martin): Problem generating structures in Nigeria's rural development, Scandinavian Inst. Of African Studies 1976 140p table. Graph. 22 cm

19. KULSHRESTA (S.K) Urban Land development policies in Nigeria: Ekistics 1976 n° 244

20. LEWIS (W.A): Réflexions sur la croissance économique du Nigéria Paris 1947 78p tabla. INSEE

21. MORGAN (W.T.W): Le Nigéria, London, New York Longmans cop 1983 XX-179p 66 fig. Photo 23cm

22. OBOLI (H.O.N): New outline geography of West Africa 8° edit. Rev. London Harraps Books Lagos 1978 143p 60 carts 25cm.

23. OFOMATA (G.E.K): Some observations on relief and erosion in eastern Nigeria-1967 n° 1 pp21-29

24. WELLS (F.A): Studies in industrialization in Nigeria and the Cameroon ed. Nigeria Inst. Of Sociology and economic Research, London 1962 266p

Books on Climate

General books on climate:

1. BELL (F.C): A survey of recent developments in rain fall runoff estimations. Inst. Eng. Annual 1966 pp 37-47 4 figs

2. CROUSE (R.P), CORBETT (E.S) & SEEGRIST (D.W): Methods of measuring and analysing rain fall interception by grass B. Assoc. Inst. Hydrology. Science. 1966 pp 110-120 7 Figs

3. YOUNG (L.H): Mean annual rainfall run off relationship. Journal, Inst. Water Eng. London 1970 n° 7 pp 423-430 1 fig.

Books on Nigeria:

1. AYOADE (J.O): A statistical analysis of rain fall over Nigeria (Tropical geography 1974 n° 39 pp 11-33 2figs 6 table. 17 carts)
2. GARNIER (B.J): Weather conditions in Nigeria climatological research service Macgill University T. 2 1967 163 p carts table
3. OJO (O): The distribution of mean monthly perceptible water vapour and annual precipitation efficiency in Nigeria, Archives Für Met. Geophysics. Bioclima. Series B. 1970 + 18 N° 3-4 pp 221-238 carts.
4. WALTER (M.W): Length of the rainy season in Nigeria-Nig. Geogr. Journal 1967 vol. N° 2 pp 123-128.

Hydrology

General Books:

1. BELL (F.C): Estimating design floods from extreme rainfall Colorado State University Hydrol. Pop Fort, Collins 1968 n° 29 53p.
2. CHATIER (M.M): Données sur la population, Paris soc. Hydrol France Comm et débits Mai 1972 23p.
3. CHEBOTAREV (A), POPOU (O.U) and KOUDELIN (B.I): Inter relation of River water and underground water during flood periods.
4. FOURNIER (F): L'érosion hydraulique et le climat B. techno. Inf. Min Agriculture. 1969 n° 327 pp 111-115 5 tables.
5. FOURNIER (F): Transports solides effectués par les cours d'eaux (B. assoc Inst. Hydrol. Scient. 1969 t. XIX n° 3 pp 7-9, 5 tables.
6. FRECAUT (R): La variabilité de l'écoulement fluvial en milieu tropical humide. Géographie 1974 T. LXXXIII n° 457 pp 241-259 2 fig.
7. FURON (Raymond): Le problème de l'eau dans le monde P. Payot—Paris 1963.
8. HOLLIS (G.E): The estimation of the hydrological impact of urbanization: An example of the use of digital stimulation in hydrology, London University College 1970 24 P.
9. KINOSITA (T) & SONDA (T): Change of runoff due to urbanization pp787-796 3 figs.

10. LEWIN (J) & MANTON (M.M.M): Welsh flood plain studies: the nature of flood plain geometry, Journal of hydrology vol. 25 p 37-50.
11. ROYER (J.M) & VACHAUD (D): Détermination directe de l'évapora-transportation et de l'infiltration par mesure des teneurs en eau et des succions B scient. Hydrol.1974 t. 19 n° 3 pp 319-333 8 Fig.
12. SHAHJAHAN (M): Factors controlling the geometry of fluvial Meanders B. assoc. Int. Hydrol scient. 1970 t. XV n° 3 pp13-24, 9 figs.

Books on Nigeria:
1. KINOLA (R.A): Food problems in Ibadan Western Nigeria. Nigerian geogr. Journal 9 (2) 1966 pp 102-113.

The reviews and publications

General Books:
1. ABOYADE (O): Revised by Jane CAROLL: Europa publication ltd. Africa south of the Sahara 1980-81, 10th Ed. England 1980, 1372 p pp 763 & 770-782, 768-769 development and planning and future prospects.
2. PINCHEMEL (P): L'analyse morphométrique des réseaux hydrographiques in comptes rendus de l'Académie des sciences T. CCXXI Paris 1950.
3. Le logement, l'Etat et les pauvres dans les villes du tiers-monde, pratique urbaine N°2 1984.

Books on Nigeria:
1. ADAMLEKUN (L) & LALEYE (M): Administration et développement au niveau local, l'expérience du Nigéria 1960-1978. Revue Française d'Administration Publique, 7 Juillet/Septembre 1978 pp. 159-186.
2. AKPAN (E.E): The development of local Government overseas. Vol. IV n° 2. April 1965 pp 118-127.
3. AVBOUBO (A.A): & OGBE (F.C.A): Geology and hydrocarbon productivity trends of southern Nigeria basin oil and gas Journal 27 November 1976 pp 48, 90, 93.

4. BJELVENSTEM (B): De la tribu à la notion. Le Nigéria et ses 40,000,000 habitants.

5. COETZEE (J.H): Peoples of Nigeria. In bulletin of Africa Institute of south Africa. Vol. 8 n° 4 May 1970 pp 135-153.

6. EKANI-ONAMBELE (Matthew): Nigéria. Progrès ou croissance? In France. Euro-Afrique n° 159 Février 1965 pp10-12.

7. Europa-France, Outre Mer: L'industrialisation du Nigéria n° 378 Mai 1961 pp 38-40.

8. Federal Ministry of Information: Nigeria handbook 1978-79 Lagos p 402.

9. Federal Ministry of Information: Niger Lagos 1960 64p photo.

10. LERAT (Serge): Vingt ans d'exploration pétrolière au Nigéria. Les cahiers d'outre mer n° 124 Octobre 1978 pp 343-358.

11. Nigéria politique coloniale Angleterre, le Nigéria du sud et les humanitaires Anglais—Bruxelles Lebeque Sd 1905 15 pp Fig.

12. OKECHUKWU MEZU (J): Du Nigéria oriental à la République du biafra in esprit n° Déc. 1969 M 787-806.

13. Problèmes (les) actuels de l'économie Nigériane. Information géographique Sept-Oct 1977, pp 180-185 table INSEE 1

14. TAVERNIER (Jacques): Au Nigéria ménac d'éclatement et de désorganisation organique l'expansion de l'économie a ravivé les particularités ethniques. In Europe France Outre Mer n° 441, Oct. 1966—pp 9-12.

15. Ten Year: Plan of development and Welfare for Nigeria, Lagos Gov. Printer 1946 153 p CEE n° 30107-Ray 37/530 (select committee of the council)

16. In notes études documentaires: Aperçu géographique n° 3154, Jan 1965 pp. 3-6.

17. In notes et études documentaires: Aperçu ethnographique et démographique n° 3154 Jan 1965—pp 11-14.

18. In l'information géographique: Pétrole (du) en Nigéria n° 5 Nov./déc. 1964. Pp.216-217.

19. In notes et études documentaires: Transport et communications n° 3154-pp 24-27.

20. Notes et études documentaires n° 3505-3506 Juillet 1968.

Reference books on the Coastal Niger Delta

1. ADAMA (N.A): A study of Amassoma community in Rivers State 1969/70. Memoir: Associate certificate in education—none published.
2. ALAGOA (E.J): A history of the Niger Delta. An interpretation of Ijo oral traditions. Ibadan 1972.
3. ALAGOA (E.J): Oral tradition among the Ijo of the Niger Delta Journal of African history Vol. 7 n° 3, 1966 417. Ijo origins and migration. Nigeria Magazine n° 91 1966 279-88.
4. ALLEN & TROTTER: Government expedition on the River Nun.
5. BAKIE (W.B): An exploring voyage into the River QUARRA and Tchadda, London 1854 page 355.
6. BLAKE (J.W): European beginning in West Africa, London 1937 pp 11-12
7. CARDI (C.N) de (compte): A short description of the natives of the Niger Coast Protectorate with some account of their customs, Religion, Trade etc.
8. CARDI (C.N) de (Compte): Juju laws and customs in the Niger Delta J.A.I XXIX 1899 pages 51-61.
9. COLE (William): Life in the Niger or the journal of an African Trader London Saunders Otley 1862 208 p.
10. DIKE (K.O): Trade and politics in the Niger Delta 1830-1885: An introduction to the economic and political history of Nigeria, Oxford 1958.
11. GRANVILLE Reginald (K) & ROTH Felix (N): Notes on the Jekris, Sabos and Ijos of the Warri District of the Niger Coast Protectorate JAI XXVII 1899 pp 104-126.
12. HORTON (J.A): West African Countries & People, London 1865 p. 171.
13. HUBBARD (J.W): The Sobo of the Niger Delta, Zaria. 1953.
14. IKIME (Oboro): Groundwork of Nigeria history ed. Heinemann, Nigeria. Ibadan 1984 615 p.
15. JEFFREYS (M.D.W): Old Calabar 1935 pp 1-22.
16. KINGSLEY (M.H): West Africa Studies. London 1899 p. 535.
17. KINGSLEY (M.H): Travels in West Africa. London 1897.
18. LANDER (Richard & John): Journal of an expedition, London 1832 III p. 176-184.

19. LEONARD (A.G): The lower Niger and its tribes London 1906 pp 17-47.

20. OJELABI (Adekunle): A textbook of West African history (1000 AD to the present day), educational research Institute Ibadan 1973 375p. pages 174-190

21. OKONKWO (D.D): History of Nigeria in New setting ed. Tabansi bookshop, Onitsha. Nigeria 1964 pp 65-68 and 72 410p.

22. OLATUNBOSUN (P.O): History of West Africa (from AD 1000 to the present day) in a correct perspective ed. Fatiregun press and publishing Company, Ilesha, Nigeria 1981 pp 165-168 340 p.

23. OWONARO (S.K): The history of Ijo-Ijaw and her neighbouring tribes in Nigeria, Lagos 1949 124p.

24. PRESTAGE (E): Tribes Portuguese pioneers, London 1938 pp 212 16.

25. TALBOT (P.A): Tribes of the Niger Delta, London 1932 p5.

26. TALBOT (P.A): Peoples of Southern Niger esp. Vols. 1 & 2. London 1926.

27. WILLIAMSON (Kay): Benue-Congo, Language and Ijo.

28. BORGHERO, FRANCESCO SAVERIO: Note géographique sur le Delta du Niger B.S.G.P th séries X (1865) pp 171-176.

29. DANGANA (L.B): Geo-Systems of the Eastern Niger Delta in Revue de géomorphologie dynamique Ed. C.D.U and CEDES réunie. Paris XXX année n° 1 1981 pp 21-27.

30. KARMON (Yehuda): A geography of settlement in Eastern Nigeria: Studies in geography Vol. XX Pamphlet n° 2 Jerusalem 1966—90 pages.

31. NEDECO: Western Niger Delta-Report on investigation the Hague 1954. 143 p.

32. NEDECO: Niger and Benue investigations, final reports 1959.

33. NEDECO: The waters of the Niger Delta: The Hague 1961 317 p.

34. SIRCAR (P.K): Problems and prospects of development of the Niger Delta, India 1972 n° 3 pp 222-236.

35. SURRE (Christian) & ZILILER (Robert): Le palmier à huile, Paris. Maisonneuve et Larousse 1963 in 8°, 271 p pl. fig., cartes, bibliographie.

36. UDO (R.K) & OGUNDANA (B): Factors influencing the fortunes of Ports in the Niger Delta. Scottish geographical magazine 1982 (3) pp 169-183, carts

Geology

References on the Coastal Niger Delta:

1. ALLEN (J.R.L): Coastal geomorphology of the Eastern Nigeria: Beach ridges, barrier Islands and vegetated tidal flats. Geol. In Mijnb 44, 1965 p 1-21.
2. ALLEN (J.R.L): Sedimentation in the Modern Delta of the River Niger, West Africa Proc Sixth interned cont. sedimentologists 1963 pp. 26-34.
3. BURKE (K): Long shore drift, submarine Canyons and submarine fans in development of the Niger Delta, Bull Amer. Assoc of petroleum geol. 56.10. 1975-10 Figs.
4. HOSPERS (J): Gravity field and structure of the Niger Delta, W.A; Bull geol. Soc. Amer 76, 1965 pp 407-422.
5. HOSPERS (J): The geology of the Niger Delta area scor. Conference, Cambridge 1970. In continental Margin (F.M. Delamy ed.) Geol. E. Atlantic H.M.S.O 1070 pp 123-142.
6. La chambre Syndicale de la recherche et de la production du pétrole du gaz naturel: Comité des techniciens: corps sédimentaires exemples sismiques et diagraphiques: éd. Technique Paris 1986 349 pp 163-182.
7. PERRODON (A): Géodynamique pétrolière: Elf Aquitaine Ed. Masson, Paris 1950 pp 329-331 (Auboubo & Obge 1978).
8. WEBER (K.J): Sediment logical aspect of oil fields in the Niger Delta-geol in Mijnb 50 1971 pp 559-576.
9. WEBER (K.J) & DOUKORU (E): Petroleum geology of the Niger Delta proc 9th World petroleum Congress, Tokyo pp 209-228, 7 figs.
10. WHITEMAN (Arthur): Nigeria: Its petroleum geology, resources and potentials ed. Graham of Trotman Ltd; London, 1982 2 vols.

SEMINARS:

1. Affaissement du sol: Gentbrugge Assoc Int. hydrol. Scient. 1970, 661 p Publ. N° 88 & 89.
2. Colloque sur l'hydrologie des Deltas UNESCO et Association Int. Hydrol. Scient. Gentbrugge 1970, 491 p Publ. N°90 & 91.
3. Dixième journée de l'hydraulique, Paris 3-5 Juillet 1968.
4. La prévision des crues et la protection contre les inondations, Paris, soc. Hydrol. France 1969 2 T 700p.

5. ONU (United Nations): Proceedings of regional symposium on flood control, reclamation utilization and development of Deltaic areas. Water resources series n° 25 Hong Kong Feb. 1954.
6. REYRE (D): Particularités géologiques de basins côtiers de l'Ouest Africain 1960, Symposium ass Serv Africaine, Paris pp 253-305: Bassins sédimentaires du Littoral Africain.

References on geography and Planning

General books:

1. ABBRAMS (A): Man's struggle for shelter in an urbanizing world, Cambridge (Mass) MIT press 1964.
2. ADRET: Construire la ville Africaine, Paris, Plan de constructions et Habitat 1984.
3. DELVERT (Jean): Notes sur la plaine de Bangkok et la zone pionnière de Kanchanaburi: Bull de l'A.G.F n° 359-350 Janvier/Février. Paris. 1968.
4. DERYCKE: L'économie urbaine: le déclin de la ville Négro-africaine.
5. DOUGLASS (Ian): The urban environment, London, Arnold, 1983.
6. DOUGLASS (I), CHANDLER (J.T) and COOKE (R.N): Physical problems of the urban environment.
7. FUNEL (J.M): Le développement régional et sa problématique, étudiés à travers l'expérience de Tahava (Niger) Paris 1976 IV, 336 p (Méthode. De la planif. 9.
8. GALLAIS (Jean): Hommes de sahel espace-temps: le Delta intérieur du Niger 1960-1980, Flammarion Cool. Géogr. 1984 286 286 P.
9. GALLAIS (Jean): Le Delta intérieur du Niger, étudie de géographie régionale 2 Vol. Daka 1967.
10. GALLAIS (Jean): La signification du village en Afrique soudanaise de l'Ouest, cahier de socio-économie II. 1960 pp 128-162.
11. GOLE (C.V) & CGITALE (S.V): Inland Delta building activity of kosi River, American Society of civil Engs. Journal of the hydraulics dimension H Y 2 111-126, 1966.
12. GOUROU (P): Le paysan du Delta Tonkinois. Etude de géographie humaine. Paris, éd. D'art et d'histoire 1936.
13. GOUROU (P): Leçon de géographie, Paris, éd. Mouton 1971.

14. HARRISON (Church): Geographical essays on British tropical lands, London, 1956.

15. HOEIKC-SMITH (M): Community participation in squatter upgrading in Zambia, Philadelphia, AFSC 1982.

16. HULL (W.R): African cities and towns before the Europeans conquest, ed. Nortow and comp. NW. 1976.

17. KUCZYNSKI (R.R): Demographic survey of the British colonial empire vol. 01I: W.A. London, Oxford University press 1948 XIII 821p Royal Inst. Of later XXXX affairs. CEE n° 26309 ray 33/416(i).

18. La société hydrotechnique de France: La prévision des crues et la protection contre les inondations 2 vols Paris 1969.

19. LEOPOLD (L.B), WOLMAN (MG) et MILLER (J): Fluvial processes in geomorphology, London 1964.

20. MARGUERAT (Y): Réflexions cursives sur l'évolution des réseaux urbains en Afrique noire. Cahier de l'O.R.S.T.O.M. Séries sciences humaine XXX 2 1978 p185.

21. MARTONNE (E): Traité de géographie physique Tome II, 4ème éd. Paris. A Colin 1926 pp. 497-1057.

22. PAYNE (G.K): Urban Housing in the third-world, London Leonard Hill 1977.

23. REXCOOP: Evaluation d'opérations d'habitat à faible coût Paris ACA 1985.

24. RIVIERES (Séré de): Le Niger, Paris 1952 p 92-94. Société d'éditions géo-maritimes et coloniales Pays Africains n° 2.

25. SILVESTER (R) & de la CRUZ (D): Pattern forming process in Delta. Journal of the Waterways and harbours, Division, American Society of Civil Eng Vol. 96 pp 201-217. 1970

26. TRICART (J): Types des fleuves et systèmes morphogénétique en Afrique occidentale: Comité travail. Inst et Scient. Paris 1955.

27. TURNER (J.F.C): Housing by people. Marion Boyars, 1976.

28. TURNER (J.F.C): Uncontrolled urban settlements: problems and solutions (document presented at the conference of United Nations, Pittsburgh) published in Braes GA (Ed). The city in newly developing countries Englewood cliffs Prentice Hall 1966 pp. 507-534

29. TURNER (J.F.C) & CAMINOS: Urban dwelling environment: MIT press 1969.